CONTENTS

Ships in Focus Publications
Correspondence and editorial:
Roy Fenton
18 Durrington Avenue
London SW20 8NT
0181 879 3527
rfenton@rfenton.demon.co.uk
Orders and photographic:
John & Marion Clarkson
18 Franklands, Longton
Preston PR4 5PD
01772 612855

Printed by Amadeus Press Ltd., Huddersfield.
Designed by Hugh Smallwood, John Clarkson and Roy Fenton.
SHIPS IN FOCUS RECORD
ISBN 1 901703 08 8

SHIPS IN FO[…] 11

A few years ago we put a sli[…] minor errors in captions de[…] photographed. One reviewe[…] that we had blundered. In […] omissions is a sign of strength rathe[…] we encourage readers to send amendments or a[…] included in 'Putting the Record Straight'. Not only does this column spur on contributors and editors to achieve even higher standards of accuracy, but it also helps ensure that errors are not perpetuated. A great strength of a journal over a book is that mistakes can be put right, so whilst doing our utmost to ensure our facts are correct and encouraging contributors to do likewise, we believe that if an error or omission gets through, the best thing is to correct it publicly. Not for nothing did we call this journal *Record.*

Having a highly observant and critical readership has rewarding, if sometimes unforeseen, results. In *Record* 10 we suggested that the counter sterns of John Holt's ships may have been unique in post-war newbuildings. Part of the rebuttal of this came in the form of Paul Boot's superb photograph of BOLIVIA on our front cover.

On a completely different matter, we have been asked by Dr. Ian Buxton to mention the Second Ship Databases Workshop, to be held at Newcastle University on Friday 30th June and Saturday 1st July 2000, whose objective is to enable users and creators of databases to share their experiences. The cost including buffet meals is £50, and further details can be obtained from Chris Deighton, Department of Marine Technology, University of Newcastle, Newcastle NE1 7RU; e-mail: chris.deighton@newcastle.ac.uk, telephone 0191 222 6171. Quite apart from the content of the meeting, this is an excellent chance to meet other researchers, and at least one of the editors of *Record* intends to be present.

John Clarkson Roy Fenton

February 2000

SUBSCRIPTION RATES FOR RECORD

VALID FROM FEBRUARY 2000

Subscribers make a saving on the postage of three issues, and receive each *Record* just as soon as it is published. They are also eligible for concessions on newly-published *Ships in Focus* titles. Readers can start their subscription with any issue, and are welcome to backdate it to receive previous issues.

UK	£23
Europe (airmail)	£25
Rest of world (surface mail)	£25 or US$41
Rest of world (airmail)	£30 or US$49

HOLMBURY: see page 134. *[World Ship Photo Library]*

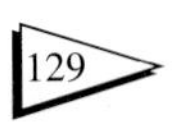

Beautifully lit by early spring sunshine, WESTBURY sails from her home port of Liverpool on 24th March 1975. Although most of their ships were registered in London, Houlders liked to have one vessel registered at each of the British ports covered by their River Plate liner service. *[Paul Boot]*

Fleet in Focus

ALEXANDER SHIPPING CO. LTD. POST-WAR

John B. Hill

Although the Alexander Shipping Co. Ltd. was established as long ago as 1914, its parent company, Capper, Alexander and Co. of Cardiff, can be traced back to 1875, when the iron clipper ships ABERMAN and ABERCARNE were built for the firm at the Stockton yard of Richardson, Duck and Co. A little later Capper, Alexander began to acquire cargo steamers and within a few years had purchased eight. However, by 1886 the fleet had been reduced to one ship and it was not until 1906 that the company began to expand again.

Following the creation of the Alexander Shipping Co. Ltd. in 1914, the first of the 'bury' boats, the WESTBURY, entered service. A succession of tramp ships were then purchased: no less than 20, all given names bearing the suffix -bury, were bought in the period between 1914 and the outbreak of the Second World War. In 1939 Alexander Shipping possessed a fleet of 13 steamers, to which was added the CHARLBURY, delivered in 1940 by the Burntisland Shipbuilding Co. Ltd. All were conventional cargo ships ranging in size from about 3,800 to 5,000 tons gross.

For the most part the ships were engaged in shipping coal from South Wales, or occasionally the north east coast, to the River Plate. Homeward cargoes were mostly grain, with some 'tween-deck space reserved for local produce such as corned beef, animal bones and hides, and hardwoods. One or two units of the fleet might have been found transporting iron ore to the United Kingdom from north or west Africa, but the South American trade predominated.

The Second World War

Few British shipping lines can have experienced such a devastating war as did Alexander Shipping. Every ship in the fleet was lost: ten being torpedoed, two sunk by German surface raiders, and one by aircraft. Perhaps the most unfortunate ship was the ASHBURY, which survived until 1945 only to be wrecked off the north coast of Scotland in January of that year whilst on passage from Loch Ewe to the River Tyne. Her entire crew of 42 was lost.

Mention might be made of one small ship which survived almost the entire period of hostilities under the management of Capper, Alexander. This was the EMPIRE SCOUT, an ex-German cargo ship of 2,229gt which, as the EILBEK, had been captured by the Royal Navy south of Iceland in November 1939. Remaining under Alexander supervision until 1946, the EMPIRE SCOUT was then sold by the Ministry of War Transport to the Dillwyn Steamship Co. Ltd., Swansea, and later found her way back to German ownership.

In addition to the EMPIRE SCOUT, a number of standard war-built Empire ships were allocated to Alexander for management during hostilities, and some of these were acquired after the war as the fleet was re-established.

The post-war years

Prior to the outbreak of war a small financial interest in the Alexander Shipping Co. Ltd. was taken up by Houlder Brothers when Alexander became a public company. This probably reflected a business relationship which existed between the two companies in finding homeward cargoes for the Alexander ships.

In 1946 Houlder Brothers, together with their parent company Furness Withy, acquired control of the Alexander Shipping Co. Ltd. and thereafter their ships were operated within the Houlder Group and adopted the Houlder funnel marking, although they retained their -bury names and flew their 'busy-bee' houseflag inferior to that of Houlder Brothers.

The re-establishment of the Alexander fleet began soon after the end of hostilities with the acquisition of six of the 12 ships which they had been managing for the Ministry of War Transport: namely EMPIRE CANYON, EMPIRE STALWART, EMPIRE BALLAD, EMPIRE GLEN, EMPIRE CLIVE and OCEAN VALLEY. Soon after purchase three of these ships, which were renamed CHARLBURY, EASTBURY and HOLMBURY, underwent major refits. They were converted from coal to oil fuel, fitted with more impressive funnels, and given much improved crew accommodation. The new 'bury' boats soon made their appearance in the South American trade but, when not required to supplement Houlder's liner services, tramping charters were arranged. For many years Houlder Brothers had operated two liner services between the United Kingdom and the River Plate: one from the west coast UK ports; the other departing from London, with occasional calls at Antwerp. London freight was usually covered by the refrigerated meat ships, which invariably terminated their homeward voyages at Royal Victoria Dock. This arrangement lead to the 'bury' ships being seen most frequently at Liverpool and in South Wales ports where they loaded general cargo, coal, and tinplate for Montevideo and Buenos Aires.

In 1947 and 1948 two Liberty ships were bought and as KINGSBURY and LEDBURY they served the Alexander fleet for 13 years, mostly in the South American trade.

A new venture for the company was the building of the NEWBURY in 1951. She was a conventional motor tanker of 16,000 tons deadweight, and entered service with an 11-year time-charter to the Shell Petroleum Co. On termination of this charter NEWBURY was sold to Finnish owners who elected not to change her name, and NEWBURY continued to trade for another ten years before being broken up in Scotland.

Replacement ships

With their general cargo fleet only comprising second-hand, standard tonnage, it was just a matter of time before the ordering of replacements was considered. In 1952 a contract was agreed for a 10,600 ton deadweight motor cargo ship with the Burntisland Shipbuilding Co. Ltd., the yard with whom Alexander had a pre-war association. Delivered in June 1953, the QUEENSBURY was in all respects a conventional cargo ship, save for her propelling machinery. Her twin, geared Gray-Polar diesel engine arrangement was chosen because it was difficult to get timely delivery of the more usual direct-drive machinery. At the time such a solution was rarely adopted for British ships, although it is now commonplace. After a few minor technical problems had been resolved, QUEENSBURY proved a most reliable addition to the fleet and she served Alexander Shipping for 18 years, almost exclusively on the Liverpool-South America route.

Whilst trade with the Argentine hardly justified expansion of the Alexander fleet, which was already operating in partnership with ships provided by Houlder Brothers, there was a pressing requirement to replace some of the standard tonnage which dated back to the early 1940s. The solution was a return to Burntisland for three cargo liners which would be rather larger than the QUEENSBURY and propelled by Doxford oil engines to give a speed of 13.5 knots. August 1958 saw the delivery of the first of the trio, the SHAFTESBURY, to be followed by the TEWKESBURY in June 1959 and the WESTBURY in November 1960. The ships were well designed for their intended trade and had accommodation for a few passengers. The engine rooms were particularly spacious and the ships proved very popular with all who sailed in them.

About this time three ships were disposed of. The CHARLBURY, EASTBURY, and HOLMBURY all went to overseas buyers for further trading. In 1960 the two Liberty ships, LEDBURY and KINGSBURY, which were the last of the standard war-time ships to be operated by Alexander Shipping, were offered for sale and both passed into Polish ownership.

Turning again to the recently built ships, an unfortunate accident befell the SHAFTESBURY in November 1959. She grounded in the River Scheldt as she was approaching Antwerp and although refloated the following day she suffered extensive damage to her bottom plating and the hull structure in way of the engine room and No. 3 hold. The main engine had been pushed up and was about 4 inches out of line. When repairs were undertaken in Rotterdam it was necessary to remove much of the machinery and renew the entire engine room double-bottom structure. To facilitate this the ship repairers adopted a novel approach. They constructed a replacement double-bottom section in the dry-dock whilst the main engine and other machinery was being removed. Then, when all the damaged structure had been cut away, about two metres of water was let into the dry-dock and this allowed the new section to be floated into position. By gradually raising the water level the new engine room double-bottom was raised to the correct height and welded into place. The whole procedure was accomplished within four weeks and the SHAFTESBURY was back in service well in advance of initial estimates.

Ships for charter

Two years after the delivery of the WESTBURY it was decided to consider the building of a faster ship which would be attractive to charterers for liner services. The outcome was another order to Burntisland in 1963, the last ship they would build for Alexander. The new ship, the TENBURY, was delivered in October 1965 and initially she was employed on the usual Liverpool-River Plate service. But as trade decreased in the late 1960s and early 1970s, TENBURY was often to be found on charter to other shipping lines, sometimes trading in the North Pacific between the United States and Japan for Japanese interests. Then in 1973 a chance attractive financial offer resulted in the TENBURY being sold, without change of name or management, to Bibby Bulk Carriers Ltd. of Liverpool. But this arrangement lasted less than a year and the ship was disposed of to Gulf Shipping (Abbas Gokal) and renamed AL-BARAT. Later she was renamed SEA EAGLE, and her demise came in April 1984 when she was struck by a missile and damaged beyond repair at Bandar Khomeini during the hostilities between Iraq and Iran.

Although the Japanese charterers of the TENBURY had indicated that they were interested in employing more ships for the United States-Japan routes, they required greater speed and ships which were container-friendly. Looking for alternatives to their traditional South American business, Alexander Shipping Co. Ltd. decided to invest in a more sophisticated vessel which would be more compliant with Japanese requirements. As a result, in 1970 a contract was placed with Scott's Shipbuilding and Engineering Co. Ltd., Greenock for an 18-knot cargo liner, equipped with deck cranes, twin hatch openings, and hydraulically-operated main and 'tween deck hatch covers. Unfortunately, during construction, the business envisaged for the ship evaporated and serious thought was given to selling her. Launched in September with an uncertain future, the BANBURY was fitting-out when a four-year bare-boat charter was secured from the Broken Hill Proprietary Co., Melbourne. To meet their requirements her name was changed to IRON BANBURY and she was registered in Newcastle. The intention was to employ the ship in the distribution of steel products to Australian coastal depots, with the occasional voyage to the Far East and Persian Gulf. There was also a requirement to transport mining equipment and rail trucks to the iron ore mining districts of north western Australia. In order to facilitate this service it was agreed to substitute one pair of the 12.5-ton hydraulic deck cranes with a pair of 25-ton capacity cranes between numbers 4 and 5 hatches. Used in tandem, this change allowed the handling of items such as rolling stock up to 50 tons.

On Christmas Day 1971, the IRON BANBURY sailed from Liverpool to Lourenco Marques for a cargo of fluorspar for discharge at Port Kembla, Newcastle, New South Wales and Whyalla. She then entered the Australian coastal trade. After four successful years in Australian waters she reverted to the name BANBURY and in a repositioning voyage she returned to the United Kingdom with a bulk cargo of grain from Port Lincoln. For a few years the BANBURY was retained by Alexander Shipping, making a series of voyages to the River Plate and occasionally being chartered to Shaw, Savill and the Pacific S.N. Co., but she did not fit well into the Houlder fleet and in 1982 she was sold to Far Eastern buyers.

It was unfortunate that the BANBURY, a fine ship and the last to be built for Alexander, did not find the niche for which she was intended. After a few years of world-wide voyaging she appears to have settled down at last, and is currently trading for the Mediterranean Shipping Co. between ports in East Africa, the Persian Gulf, and India. At 28 years of age she is unlikely to be afloat much longer but today, as the MSC ELENA, she is the last remaining link with Capper, Alexander, a shipping enterprise founded back in 1875.

The Alexander Shipping Co. Ltd. was eventually wound up in 1990, although in later years its activities were restricted to providing a vehicle for the registration of some of Houlder Brothers bulk carriers and oil tankers.

Believed to be at Port Kembla, IRON BANBURY is in the colours of the Broken Hill Proprietary Co. *[Author's collection]*

Post-war fleet list

1. AYLESBURY 1945-1948
O.N. 168682 6,327g 4,592n 420.0 x 54.7 x 33.2 feet.
T. 3-cyl. by David Rowan and Co. Ltd., Glasgow; 10 knots.
24.5.1941: Launched by Charles Connell and Co. Ltd., Scotstoun (Yard No. 433).
7.7.1941: Completed for the Ministry of War Transport, London (Clark and Service, Glasgow, managers) as EMPIRE GLEN.
1944: Managers became Capper, Alexander and Co., London.
1945: Acquired by the Alexander Shipping Co. Ltd. (Capper, Alexander and Co., managers), London and renamed AYLESBURY.
1947: Managers became Houlder Brothers and Co. Ltd.
1948: Sold to West Wales Steamship Co. Ltd. (Gibbs and Co., managers), Newport and renamed WEST WALES.
1960: Sold to the Iranian Lloyd Co. Ltd., Teheran, Iran and renamed PERSIAN XERXES.
9.1964: Sold to Frank Rijsdijk for demolition at Hendrik-Ido-Ambacht, Holland.

AYLESBURY. *[Author's collection]*

CHARLBURY with a deck cargo of buses. *[Author's collection]*

2. CHARLBURY 1946-1958.
O.N. 168801 7,069g 5,194n 447.6 x 56.2 x 34.2 feet.
T. 3-cyl. by Cammell, Laird and Co. Ltd., Birkenhead; 10 knots.
28.7.1941: Launched by Cammell, Laird and Co. Ltd., Birkenhead.(Yard No. 1060).
8.1941: Completed for the Ministry of War Transport (Capper, Alexander and Co., managers), London as the CAM ship EMPIRE CLIVE.
8.5.1946: Sold to Alexander Shipping Co. Ltd. (Capper, Alexander and Co., managers), London and renamed CHARLBURY.
1947: Managers became Houlder Brothers and Co. Ltd.
1958: Sold to Red Anchor Line Ltd. (Moller and Co.), Hong Kong and renamed ISABEL ERICA.
1964: Owners became St. Merryn Shipping Co. Ltd. (Red Anchor Line Ltd., managers), Hong Kong.
4.8.1969: Arrived at Hong Kong for demolition by Ming Hing and Co.

3. EASTBURY 1946-1958
O.N. 168956 7,045g 4,845n 446.4 x 56.3 x 26.8 feet.
T. 3-cyl. by Central Marine Engine Works, Hartlepool; 10 knots.
23.3.1943: Launched by William Gray and Co. Ltd., West Hartlepool (Yard No. 1147).
5.1943: Completed for the Ministry of War Transport (Capper, Alexander and Co., managers), London as EMPIRE STALWART.
1946: Acquired by Alexander Shipping Co. Ltd. (Capper, Alexander and Co., managers), London and renamed EASTBURY.
1947: Managers became Houlder Brothers and Co. Ltd.
1958: Sold to Transportacion Maritima Mexicana, Mexico City, Mexico and renamed CONSTITUCION.
2.7.1968: Arrived at Vera Cruz, Mexico to be broken up.

4. BIBURY 1946-1951
O.N. 169013 6,700g 4,821n 432.0 x 56.6 x 34.0 feet.
T. 3-cyl. by North Eastern Marine Engineering Co. (1938) Ltd., Sunderland; 10 knots.
17.12.41: Launched by Bartram and Sons Ltd., Sunderland (Yard No. 290).
13.3.1942: Completed for the Ministry of War Transport (Allan, Black and Co., managers), London as EMPIRE BALLAD.
1944: Managers became Capper, Alexander and Co.
1946: Acquired by the Alexander Shipping Co. Ltd. (Capper, Alexander and Co., managers), London.
1947: Managers became Houlder Brothers and Co. Ltd. and renamed BIBURY.
1951: Sold to Halcyon-Lijn N.V., Rotterdam, Holland and renamed STAD MAASLUIS.
1962: Sold to Compania de Naviera Jaguar Line S.A., Panama (Palomba and Salvatori, Naples, Italy) and renamed JAGUAR.
1966: Renamed GOLDFIELD.
1968: Sold to Compania de Naviera Solemar, Panama (V. Coccoli, Naples, Italy) and renamed POSEIDONE.
6.1969: Grounded whilst on passage from Rouen to Alexandria with a cargo of grain.
15.9.1969: Arrived at Naples and condemned.
21.11.1969: Arrived in tow at Split to be broken up by Brodospas.

5. HOLMBURY 1946-1960
O.N. 166216 7,058n 4,871n 446.3 x 56.3 x 35.2 feet.
T. 3-cyl. by North Eastern Marine Engineering Co. (1938) Ltd., Wallsend-on-Tyne; 10 knots.
11.11.1943: Launched by Caledon Shipbuilding and Engineering Co. Ltd., Dundee (Yard No. 408).
12.1943: Completed for the Ministry of War Transport (F.C. Strick and Co. Ltd., managers), London as EMPIRE CANYON.
1946: Acquired by the Alexander Shipping Co. Ltd. (Capper, Alexander and Co., managers), London.
1947: Managers became Houlder Brothers and Co. Ltd. and renamed HOLMBURY.
1960: Sold to United Orient Steamship Co., Karachi, Pakistan and renamed ILYASBAKSH.
12.8.1965: Arrived at Bombay from Cochin and interned by India during hostilities between India and Pakistan.
11.1966: Arrested.
10.1970: Sold to Najabali and Co. for demolition.
12.1970: Work commenced at Bombay.

BIBURY. *[Author's collection]*

EASTBURY sailing from Swansea (above).

HOLMBURY on 6th July 1951 (below). *[F.W. Hawks]*

The Liberty-type KINGSBURY: note the non-standard wheelhouse. *[Fotoflite incorporating Skyfotos]*

6. KINGSBURY 1947-1960
O.N. 180533 7,246g 4,415n 441.7 x 57.1 x 34.8 feet.
T. 3-cyl. by General Machinery Corporation, Hamilton, Ontario, Canada; 11 knots.
14.6.1944: Launched by Bethlehem-Fairfield Shipyard Inc., Baltimore, Maryland, USA (Yard No. 2378) for the United States War Shipping Administration, New York, USA as SAMLAMU.
6.1944: Completed and bare-boat chartered to the Ministry of War Transport, London (Sir William Reardon Smith and Sons Ltd., Cardiff, managers).
4.1947: Acquired by the Alexander Shipping Co. Ltd. (Houlder Brothers and Co. Ltd., managers), London and renamed KINGSBURY.
1960: Sold to Polska Zegluga Morska, Szczecin, Poland and renamed HUTA BEDZIN.
1969: Converted into a floating storage hulk for Zarzad Portu Gdynia and renamed MP-ZP-GDY-6.
7.1982: Arrived at Hamina, Finland to be broken up by Haminan Laivaromu O/Y.

7. LEDBURY 1948-1961
O.N. 169652 7,265g 4,456n 441.7 x 57.0 x 34.8 feet.
T. 3-cyl. by General Machinery Corporation, Hamilton, Ontario, Canada; 11 knots.
27.9.1943: Launched by Bethlehem-Fairfield Shipyard Inc., Baltimore, Maryland, USA (Yard No. 2242) for the United States War Shipping Administration, New York, USA as JOHN RUSSELL POPE.
10.1943: Completed and bare-boat chartered to the Ministry of War Transport, London (Moss Hutchison Line Ltd., Liverpool, managers) as SAMDAK.
4.1947: Sold to Alpha South African Steamship Co. Ltd., London (Moller Lines S.A. (Pty.) Ltd., Durban) and renamed ALPHA VAAL.
5.1948: Acquired by the Alexander Shipping Co. Ltd. (Houlder Brothers and Co. Ltd., managers), London and renamed LEDBURY.
1961: Sold to Polska Zegluga Morska, Szczecin, Poland and renamed KOPALPNA CZELADZ.
21.2.1973: Arrived at Faslane for demolition by Shipbreaking Industries Ltd.

In contrast to KINGSBURY, LEDBURY had a standard Liberty wheelhouse. *[Fotoflite incorporating Skyfotos]*

The Ocean-type MALMESBURY. *[A. Duncan]*

8. MALMESBURY 1949-1955
O.N. 168556 7,174g 4,272n 441.5 x 57.0 x 34.8 feet.
T. 3-cyl. by General Machinery Corporation, Hamilton, Ontario, Canada; 11 knots.
9.12.1941: Launched by the Todd-California Shipbuilding Corporation, Richmond, California, USA (Ship No. 7).
1.1942: Completed for the Ministry of War Transport (Capper, Alexander and Co., managers), London as OCEAN VALLEY.
1949: Acquired by the Alexander Shipping Co. Ltd. (Houlder Brothers and Co. Ltd., managers), London and renamed MALMESBURY.
1955: Sold to Trafalgar Steamship Co. Ltd. (Tsavliris (Shipping) Ltd.), London and renamed GRANNY SUZANNE.
1958: Owners became the Nigean Shipping Co. S.A., Panama (Tsavliris (Shipping) Ltd., London) and renamed FREE ENTERPRISE under the Liberian flag.
1958: Renamed ALEXANDROS TSAVLIRIS.
1964: Owners became Trafalgar Steamship Co. Ltd., (Tsavliris (Shipping) Ltd.), London and renamed NEWDENE.
1965: Owners became Kantara Shipping Co. Ltd., Limassol, Cyprus (Tsavliris (Shipping) Ltd., London) and renamed FREE NAVIGATOR.
1.7.1969: Arrived at La Spezia, in tow from Kynosoura, where she had been laid up since November 1968, for demolition by Cantieri Navali Del Golfo S.p.A.
12.1969: Demolition commenced.

9. NEWBURY 1951-1963 Tanker
O.N. 184535 11,199g 6,482n 530.3 x 68.2 x 37.2 feet.
Rowan-Doxford oil engine 5-cyl. 2SCSA by David Rowan and Co. Ltd., Glasgow; 5,500bhp, 13.5 knots.
7.1951: Launched by Lithgows Ltd., Port Glasgow (Yard No. 1060) for Alexander Shipping Co. Ltd. (Houlder Brothers and Co. Ltd., managers), London as NEWBURY.
12.1951: Completed.
1963: Sold to Angfartygs A/B Alfa (Lundqvist-Rederierna, managers), Mariehamn, Finland.
20.8.1973: Arrived at Faslane for demolition by Shipbreaking Industries Ltd.

The motor tanker NEWBURY. *[Peter Kenyon collection]*

QUEENSBURY

Trials shots of SHAFTESBURY (above) and TEWKESBURY (below). *[Both: Author's collection]*

10. QUEENSBURY 1953-1971
O.N. 185900 6,175g 3,415n 457.1 x 59.8 x 26.7 feet
Two Gray-Polar oil engines each 6-cyl. 2SCSA geared to one shaft by Central Marine Engine Works, Hartlepool; 4,664 bhp, 12.5 knots.
16.3.1953: Launched by the Burntisland Shipbuilding Co. Ltd., Burntisland (Yard No. 350) for Alexander Shipping Co. Ltd. (Houlder Brothers and Co. Ltd., managers), London as QUEENSBURY.
6.1953: Completed.
1971: Sold to Kyknos Shipping Co. Ltd., Famagusta, Cyprus (Transmarine Shipping Agencies Ltd., London) and renamed SANDRA.
1973: Sold to Shun Fong Maritime S.A., Panama (Lai Ching Yu, Taipei, Taiwan) and renamed FONG LEE.
1976: Sold to Lien Chang Navigation Co. Ltd., Hong Kong and renamed LIEN CHANG under the Panama flag.
18.11.1978: Arrived at Kaohsiung and subsequently broken up by Swie Horng Steel Enterprise Co.

11. SHAFTESBURY 1958-1972
O.N. 187839 8,532g 4,799n 457.0 x 62.0 x 28.8 feet.
Hawthorn-Doxford oil engine 5-cyl. 2SCSA by Hawthorn, Leslie (Engineers) Ltd., Newcastle-upon-Tyne; 5,500bhp, 13 knots.
4.4.1958: Launched by Burntisland Shipbuilding Co. Ltd., Burntisland (Yard No. 382) for the Alexander Shipping Co. Ltd. (Houlder Brothers and Co. Ltd., managers), London as SHAFTESBURY.
8.1958: Completed.
1972: Sold to First United Carriers Inc., Panama (Del Bene Ultramar S.A.C.I.F., Buenos Aires, Argentina) and renamed PORTLOE.
1973: Renamed ARAUCO.
1976: Owners became Compania Chilena de Naviera Interoceanica, Valparaiso, Chile.
1978: Sold to Fife Shipping Co. Ltd., Panama (Transglobe Maritime Ltd., Hong Kong) and renamed JAL SEA CONDOR.
3.7.1978: Sprang a leak off Cunene River, Angola in position 16.55 south by 11.25 east and abandoned whilst on passage from Bangkok to Lagos with 8,000 tons of rice and general cargo.
6.7.1978: Sank in position 19.10 south by 12.08 east whilst in tow for Walvis Bay.

12. TEWKESBURY 1959-1972
O.N. 300929 8,532g 4,792n 457.0 x 62.0 x 28.9 feet
Hawthorn-Doxford oil engine 5-cyl. 2SCSA by Hawthorn, Leslie (Engineers) Ltd., Newcastle-upon-Tyne; 5,500bhp, 13 knots.
25.3.1959: Launched by the Burntisland Shipbuilding Co. Ltd., Burntisland (Yard No. 388) for the Alexander Shipping Co. Ltd. (Houlder Brothers and Co. Ltd., managers), London as TEWKESBURY.
6.1959: Completed.
1972: Sold to Del Bene Ultramar S.A.C.I.F., Buenos Aires, Argentina and renamed CAMINITO.
1981: Sold to Colbrook Shipping Corporation, Monrovia, Liberia (European Navigation Inc., S. Karnessis and D. Vlassakis, Piraeus, Greece) and renamed BRAZIL under the Panama flag.
7.1984: Broken up by Golden Sea International, Bangkok, Thailand.

13. WESTBURY 1960-1978
O.N. 301362 8,533g 4,788n 457.0 x 62.0 x 28.9 feet.
Hawthorn-Doxford oil engine 5-cyl. 2SCSA by Hawthorn, Leslie (Engineers) Ltd., Newcastle-upon-Tyne; 5,500bhp, 13 knots.
11.5.1960: Launched by the Burntisland Shipbuilding Co. Ltd., Burntisland (Yard No. 401) for the Alexander Shipping Co. Ltd. (Houlder Brothers and Co. Ltd., managers), London as WESTBURY.
11.1960: Completed.
1978: Sold to National Glory Compania Naviera S.A., Panama (Canopus Shipping S.A., Andreas and George Kyrtatas, Athens, Greece) and renamed DIAMONDO under the Greek flag.
1980: Sold to the Iktinos Shipping Co. (Intermarine Ltd., K. Koukoulas and A. Nikoloulias), Piraeus, Greece and renamed POLANA.
24.5.1983: Arrived at Gadani Beach for demolition by the Mercantile Trading Co.

14. TENBURY 1965-1973
O.N. 307940 8,459g 4,717n 462.0 x 63.0 x 29.0 feet.
John Brown-Sulzer oil engine 6-cyl. 2SCSA by John Brown and Co. (Clydebank) Ltd., Clydebank; 9,467bhp, 16 knots.
14.5.1965: Launched by the Burntisland Shipbuilding Co. Ltd., Burntisland (Yard No. 409) for the Alexander Shipping Co. Ltd. (Houlder Brothers and Co. Ltd., managers), London as TENBURY.
4.10.1965: Completed.
1973: Sold to Bibby Bulk Carriers Ltd., Liverpool (Houlder Brothers and Co. Ltd., London, managers).
1974: Sold to Boundary Bay Shipping Co. Ltd., Monrovia, Liberia (Gulfeast Ship Management, A.K.and M.K. Gokal, Karachi, Pakistan) and renamed AL-BARAT.
1980: Sold to the Arabian Maritime Transport Co. Ltd (Saudi Research and Development Corporation, Jeddah) (Gulf Ship Management Ltd., Hong Kong and Karachi, managers) and renamed SEA EAGLE.
27.4.1984: Struck by an Exocet missile fired by an Iraqi aircraft in the Khor Musa channel whilst on passage from Tunisia to Bandar Khomeini with a cargo of fertiliser. The cargo was discharged, but the vessel was damaged beyond repair.
10.12.1984: Demolition began at Alang, India by the Metal Scrap Trade Corporation Ltd.

TENBURY on trials. *[Author's collection]*

15. BANBURY 1971-1982
O.N. 337373 11,381g 6,678n 525.0 x 75.0 x 43.0 feet.
Scott-Sulzer oil engine 7 cyl. 2SCSA by Scott's Engineering Co. (1969) Ltd., Greenock; 14,000bhp, 18 knots.
19.9.1971: Launched by Scott's Shipbuilding Co. (1969) Ltd., Greenock (Yard No. 721) for the Alexander Shipping Co. Ltd. (Houlder Brothers and Co. Ltd., managers), London as BANBURY (registered at Newcastle-upon-Tyne).
17.12.1971: Delivered as IRON BANBURY for a four-year bare-boat charter to the Broken Hill Pty. Co. Ltd., Melbourne, Australia.
1975: Renamed BANBURY.
1982: Sold to Onward Maritime Inc., Panama (Wallem Shipmanagement Ltd., Hong Kong) and renamed LADY MARINA..
1989: Sold to Compania Naviera Ariane S.A., Panama (Mediterranean Shipping Co. S.A., Geneva, Switzerland) and renamed ARIANE S.
1992: Renamed PRESIDENTE AGUIRRE CERDA.
1994: Renamed MSC ELENA
Still in service (11.1999).

Vessels operated by Houlder Brothers and Co. Ltd., but registered under the ownership of the Alexander Shipping Co. Ltd., London.

A. UPWEY GRANGE 1976-198 B-26-type bulk carrier
O.N. 366139 15,903g 1,1082n 183.0 x 22.8 x 10.47 meters.
Clark NEM-Sulzer oil engine 6-cyl. 2SCSA by G. Clark and N.E.M Ltd., Wallsend-on-Tyne; 9,900bhp, 15 knots.
3.3.1976: Launched by Austin and Pickersgill Ltd., South Dock, Sunderland (Yard No 902) for the Alexander Shipping Co. Ltd. (Houlder Brothers and Co. Ltd., managers), London as UPWEY GRANGE (originally to have been named AYLESBURY).
1976: Completed.
1982: Sold to Ace Pacific Navigation Co., Panama (Fuyo Sogo Lease K.K., Tokyo, Japan) and renamed LILY VILLAGE.
1987: Sold to Cartron Overseas Inc., Panama (Seama International Shipping, V.N. Mavreas, London) and renamed PUGGI.
1990: Sold to Congress Shipping Co. Ltd., Limassol, Cyprus (Transcontinental Maritime and Trading S.A., Piraeus, Greece), and renamed NATALIA.
1991: Owners became Observer Shipping Co. Ltd., Limassol, Cyprus (Transcontinental Maritime and Trading S.A., Piraeus, Greece) and renamed RANGER.
1995: Sold to Orgullo Navigation Ltd., Panama (Allied Maritime Inc., Athens, Greece) and renamed ORGULLO.
Still in service (11.1999).

B. LYNTON GRANGE 1976-1982 B-26-type bulk carrier
O.N. 366279 15,903g 11,082n 183.04 x 22.84 x 10.478 meters.
Hawthorn-Sulzer oil engine 6-cyl. 2SCSA by Hawthorn, Leslie (Engineers) Ltd., Newcastle-upon-Tyne; 9,900bhp, 15 knots.
12.5.1976: Launched by Austin and Pickersgill Ltd., Southwick, Sunderland (Yard No 903) for the Alexander Shipping Co. Ltd. (Houlder Brothers and Co. Ltd., managers), London as LYNTON GRANGE.
1976: Completed.
1982: Sold to Central Shipping (Holdings) Inc., Panama (Fuyo Sogo Lease K.K., Tokyo, Japan) and renamed NORTHERN CHERRY.
1990: Sold to Chios Charm Shipping Co. S.A., Panama (Harbour Shipping and Trading S.A., Chios, Greece) and renamed CHIOS CHARM.
Still in service (11.1999).

C. HORNBY GRANGE 1979-1984 Tanker
O.N. 379972 39,626g 25,730n 228.28 x 32.26 x 13.3 meters.
Burmeister & Wain oil engine 6-cyl. 2SCSA by Harland and Wolff Ltd., Belfast; 20,500bhp, 16 knots.
5.10.1978: Launched by Harland and Wolff Ltd. (Yard No. 1709) for the Alexander Shipping Co. Ltd. (Houlder Brothers and Co. Ltd., managers), London as HORNBY GRANGE.
1979: Completed.
1984: Owners became Shaw Savill and Albion Co. Ltd., London.
1985: Sold to Fest Atlantic Co., Monrovia and renamed SANTA BARBARA.
1989: Sold to Transpetrol Nav. Pte. Ltd., Singapore (Transpetrol Services N.V., Brussels, Belgium) and renamed AFFINITY.
11.1999: Sold Greek owners.
Still in service (11.1999).

D. ELSTREE GRANGE 1979-1984 Tanker
O.N 39,626g 2,5730n 228.25 x 32.31 x 13.301 meters.
Burmeister & Wain oil engine 6-cyl. 2SCSA by Harland and Wolff Ltd., Belfast; 20,500bhp, 16 knots.
26.1.1979: Launched by Harland and Wolff Ltd. (Yard No. 1710) for the Alexander Shipping Co. Ltd. (Houlder Brothers and Co. Ltd., managers), London as ELSTREE GRANGE.
10.1979: Completed.
1984: Owners became Shaw Savill and Albion Co. Ltd., London.
1985: Sold to Fest Pacific Co. Ltd., Monrovia (C.H. Tung, Hong Kong) and renamed SANTA LUCIA.
1989: Sold to White Tankers Private Ltd., Singapore (Transpetrol Services N.V., Brussels, Belgium) and renamed SPIRIT.
11.1999: Sold Greek owners.
Still in service (11.1999).

E. OROTAVA BRIDGE/RIPON GRANGE 1978-1979 Ore carrier
O.N. 334768 28,880g 20,614n 716.3 x 92.3 x 41.2 feet
Doxford oil engine 6-cyl. 2SCSA by Sunderland Shipbuilders Ltd., Sunderland.
3.11.1967: Completed by Doxford and Sunderland Shipbuilding and Engineering Co. Ltd. - Sir James Laing, Sunderland (Yard No. 842) for Ore Carriers Ltd. (Houlder Brothers and Co. Ltd.), London as OROTAVA.
2.1968: Completed.
1969: Renamed OROTAVA BRIDGE.
1974: Renamed OROTAVA.
1978: Owners became the Alexander Shipping Co. Ltd., London.
1979: Renamed RIPON GRANGE.
1979: Owners became Furness Withy and Co. Ltd. (Houlder Brothers and Co. Ltd.), London.
1980: Sold to Leda Segundo Cia. Nav. S.A., Panama (S. Stravelakis, Piraeus, Greece) and renamed LEDA under the Greek flag.
1982: Owners became Unity Enterprises Co. Ltd., Valletta, Malta (S. Stravelakis, Piraeus, Greece) and renamed UNITY.
1984: Owners became Romneya Shipping Corporation, Monrovia, Liberia (S. Stravelakis, Piraeus, Greece) and renamed LATINI under the Greek flag.
About 25.4.1986: Arrived in China for demolition.

Note: In accordance with their details in *Lloyd's Register,* the Alexander ships are shown as being managed by Houlder Brothers and Co. Ltd. from 1947. In practice, the day-to-day management of the ships was in the hands of Alexander Shipping's own office, within the ship management department of Houlder Brothers.

BANBURY (top). *[Author's collection]*

UPWEY GRANGE (upper middle). *[World Ship Photo Library]*

ELSTREE GRANGE fitting out at Belfast (lower middle). *[World Ship Photo Library]*

The OROTAVA is seen here on 18th August 1971 as OROTAVA BRIDGE (bottom). Towards the end of her career with Houlder Brothers, OROTAVA was briefly registered in the ownership of Alexander Shipping Co. Ltd.

THE POTATO SHIP THAT TURNED TURTLE

Dave Hocquard and Robert Le Maistre

The JOHN V was built in 1938 in Martenshoek by Bodewes Scheepswerven as the LENA for Zeevaart Maats, Zaandam. She had a gross tonnage of 383, a deadweight of 450 and net of 177. Principal dimensions were 136.8 feet overall, 24.7 feet beam with a maximum draft of 10.5 feet. Power was supplied by a six-cylinder four-stroke Deutz oil engine giving a maximum speed of nine knots.

LENA worked mainly in the timber trade until the outbreak of the Second World War. Her first recorded movement during the war was at the evacuation of the British Expeditionary Force from Dunkirk where, under the command of Lieutenant-Commander R. Hawkins RN Retired, LENA is reported to have rescued 996 men. However, on 4th June 1940 she had the misfortune to be abandoned on the beach at La Panne along with three other Dutch motor coasters and was listed by the Admiralty as lost. She was subsequently refloated and returned to service by the Germans. According to a General Order to the German Naval Commander Channel Coast dated 24th October 1941, the LENA was based at Cherbourg as a supply ship for the Channel Islands, serving mainly Alderney and she appears in a photograph of Braye Harbour, taken before the German jetty was built in mid-1942 with the tug FK01 alongside, this vessel later becoming the States of Jersey tug DUKE OF NORMANDY.

After D-Day and the American advance around the Gulf of St. Malo the LENA was laid up in St. Aubins Harbour, Jersey. She finally sailed on the evening tide of 27th May 1945 for St. Helier where she remained until 11th July when she sailed for Southampton to be returned to her former owners.

Potatoes from Jersey

After the war LENA resumed her former trade and in 1951 was sold to International Shipbrokers of Rotterdam, renamed JOHN V and put under the British flag. Her first visit to Jersey was on 21st June 1951 when she arrived from Teignmouth to load a cargo of potatoes for Portsmouth. On lst July the JOHN V again arrived light, from Portsmouth, for the first time under the command of Captain J. Hughes. The ship lay over on the 'Bank', Albert Quay, until her cargo of potatoes was loaded during 3rd July.

At 10.00pm the same day, on a calm summer's evening, the JOHN V, under the guidance of the local pilot George Guille, left St. Helier Harbour bound for Portsmouth with a cargo of 398 tons of potatoes, 363 tons of which were below hatches with the remaining 35 tons on deck. It was noted as she departed through the Pierheads that she had a slight list to port but this was not considered unusual or of any consequence. On the bridge Captain Hughes and the mate were discussing who was to take the watch, while the helmsman, ordinary seaman J. Van der Vaart, received instructions from the pilot. The chief officer Chute-Neligan, who was married to a local girl living at Cromarty Lodge, Green Island, signalled 'goodnight' by torch flashes to his wife as was his usual custom when leaving Jersey. After a short while the ship started to turn on to the leading lights, just past the La Platte Beacon, when suddenly a heavy list to port developed. The helmsman immediately tried to bring the ship back on an even keel but to no avail. The ship continued to go over and pilot Guille, on seeing what was happening, made every effort to bring her round to clear the traffic in this the main approach to St. Helier and, going right over on to her port side, the JOHN V ended up with her bow facing St. Aubins. Down in the engine room Chief Engineer P.H. Mitchell had felt the ship list badly and when things started crashing around him abandoned the engine room to find the ship rapidly turning turtle.

Eric de Gruchy, on the pilot cutter MARIE, which had been waiting to take off Guille, saw what was happening and skilfully manoeuvred the cutter alongside the ship as she turned and when she was half way over took the crew off as they slid down the ship's side on a rope. With the ship right over the pilot and others abandoned ship by walking down the side of the bridge, then sliding along the hull until they reached the bilge chocks after which they stepped on to the pilot cutter without even getting their feet wet! The ship had turned turtle so quickly that the propeller was still turning.

The first news received on land of the casualty was when an officer from the ship landed on the quay and told the pierhead watchman. Immediately the Harbour Office was notified of the disaster the Harbour Master and his deputy went out to the wreck, now in a positon half a mile west-south-west of the La Platte Beacon, aboard the cutter MAJOR PIERSON. Their main concern was that the wreck should not become a hazard to shipping so a rope was fixed to the propeller aperture of the JOHN V and led to the MFV ADRAIA which was also at the scene. The ADRAIA together with the MAJOR PIERSON and the pilot cutter MARIE started to tow the wreck towards the beach at St. Aubins. It was now close to low water and the tow was made even more difficult by the masts of the JOHN V snagging on the seabed until they eventually broke off. This made the tow easier and as the tide rose the JOHN V was well up into the bay towards First Tower. The crew, now ashore, had been found accommodation while Captain Hughes and Mr. Renouf, the ships agent, remained at the wreck all night aboard the ADRAIA.

JOHN V (above). *[Fotoflite incorporating Skyfotos]*

JOHN V is seen below on 4th July 1951 lying on her side in St. Aubins Bay near to low tide. Sacks of potatoes can be seen washing out of her hold. *[Jersey Evening Post]*

Salvage

By light of day part of the cargo of potatoes together with pieces of flotsam and wreckage could be seen floating in St. Aubins Bay, most of the cargo, however, was still in the holds. The wreck was now lying with her bow pointing eastwards and her propeller well clear of the water.

The most important matter now was salvage. On the morning of 5th July a representative of a salvage insurance company and an official of the company owning the JOHN V went out to inspect the wreck, returning to it during the afternoon. By this time the wheelhouse had broken away from the hull and the holds were practically empty. Such was the attraction of the wreck that people rowed out to her, the more adventurous of them climbing aboard. As a result, the ship's agent placed a warning in the *Jersey Evening Post* stating that any unauthorised person found aboard the JOHN V or removing articles from her would be liable for prosecution. The wreck proved such an attraction that on a number of occasions the motor launch SKYLON operated trips

Afloat again, JOHN V is taken in tow by the French tug ABEILLE No 3 on 13th July 1951 (right). *[Jersey Evening Post]*

The damaged JOHN V leaves St. Helier for Rotterdam in tow of the ABEILLE No. 10 on 18th July 1951 (below). *[Jersey Evening Post]*

from the Albert Quay to view it.

On the evening of 5th July representatives of the French salvage company La Société de Remorque et de Sauvetage (Les Abeilles, Le Havre) arrived in Jersey by air from Le Havre and during 6th July carried out an inspection of the wreck. By Sunday 8th July the French salvage vessel FRANCOIS QUERE and the French tug ABEILLE No 3 had arrived in St. Aubins Bay and commenced the task of salvaging the wreck. These two vessels were joined on the following day by another French salvage vessel, the MARIE MADELEINE, which arrived direct from Dunkirk.

Despite unfavourable weather conditions and a heavy swell in St. Aubins Bay, the JOHN V was righted by Thursday 12th July and was completely afloat the following day. The righting had been effected by placing wires under the wreck and, with all vents and other places likely to admit water plugged, the vessel was slowly brought on to an even keel by a combination of lifting and hauling by the salvage vessels. Pumps were used to pump out the wreck and, as the water level decreased, buoyancy increased, thereby helping the righting. During the morning on Friday 13th July the JOHN V was secured to the ABEILLE No. 3. After a thorough survey by representatives of the owners, the salvage association, and her local agents, the tow from St. Aubins Bay to St. Helier Harbour commenced shortly after 1.15pm, the FRANCOIS QUERE remaining close by. The JOHN V arrived in St. Helier Harbour at 1.44pm and was berthed on the New North Quay. A terrible smell of rotting potatoes in salt water was noticeable on the ship and had been evident around St. Aubins Bay for several days.

Repairing the damage

The damage to the ship was less than expected. Her bridge and wheelhouse were missing as well as her masts and ventilators but the latter two had been salvaged and were on one of the salvage vessels. The funnel, binnacle and steering wheel were still present with damage to the port side bulkwarks and the port side of the superstructure aft evident. The machinery appeared to have suffered little damage.

During the course of the following days the JOHN V's holds, engine room and accommodation were cleaned up and the ship made seaworthy. On 18th July the French tug ABEILLE No 10 arrived from Le Havre and at 6.50pm departed for Rotterdam with the JOHN V lashed alongside.

After repairs and a refit the JOHN V resumed her trading activities but was never again seen in Jersey. From 1952, however, she did operate for at least two seasons carrying tomatoes from Guernsey to Belfast. In 1956 she was sold to J.J. de Looff of Oosterhogebrug, renamed MUSKETIER and her port of registry changed to Groningen. She traded without incident until 2nd November 1962 when, whilst on passage from Dunkirk to Perth with fertilizer, she went aground off Crail in the Tay Estuary, Fife and became a total loss. The crew were rescued by the Anstruther lifeboat.

What went wrong?

Let us now return to the sinking in St. Aubins Bay and consider the cause. We have found no evidence of any Court of Enquiry so let us consider the most likely cause of the JOHN V turning turtle. The first question is, was she overloaded? The answer is no. Her deadweight tonnage was 450 tons, 24 tons of which was bunkers and approximately 2 to 3 tons of stores. On the night in question the JOHN V was carrying a total cargo of 398 tons, 363 of which were below decks in her two holds with the remaining 35 tons being carried on deck. Obviously she was top heavy, so the next question is, was she carrying too much cargo on deck? Again the answer is no for when carrying timber she would have approximately 50 tons on deck. So what did go wrong?

When a coaster makes a voyage without cargo she takes on water ballast in both her forward and aft peak tanks and also in her double bottom tanks in order to give her a good trim and to keep her propeller as deep in the water as possible. On starting to load the water ballast would be pumped out and on completion of loading water ballast would be pumped back into some tanks, particularly if deck cargo is being carried, in order to maintain trim and a low centre of gravity. It seems posible, therefore, that in the case of the JOHN V this was not done, thereby making her top heavy and very tender.

While manoeuvering in the harbour at slow speed there was no problem but once clear of the Pierheads she would have worked up to her full service speed of around eight knots. On turning to starboard to round the La Platte Beacon she heeled slightly and, being unable to recover, continued to roll over although fortunately with no loss of life.

Just over a year after turning turtle, JOHN V loads tomatoes for Belfast at St. Peter Port, Guernsey (right). *[Dave Hocquard]*

JOHN V in later life as MUSKETIER (below). *[Roy Fenton collection]*

BAZELEYS OF PENZANCE AND THE LITTLE WESTERN STEAMSHIP COMPANY

Part two

Tony Pawlyn

During 1884 Bazeleys acquired the first of what was, for them, a new class of cargo liner in the form of the GERVASE. Completed in 1880, she had much greater cargo capacity than existing ships. With engines amidships, and a long raised quarterdeck, with full 'tween decks for the stowage of lighter parcels, her deep hull had a greatly increased freeboard. She had deck cranes fore and aft, and Bazeleys' advertisements credited the GERVASE as carrying 700 tons.

Registered at Penzance on 15th October 1884, she was placed under the command of Captain Hodge, with the now customary seniority shuffle running down through the other vessels. To raise the capital to pay for this new steamer Bazeleys took out a mortgage with the Penzance banker Richard Foster Bolitho for £4,500.

On Tuesday 12th November 1884 the GERVASE had the distinction of being the first merchant vessel to enter the new docks at Penzance in the normal course of trade. The ceremony of opening the new dock had taken place the previous day, when Bazeleys' THAMES took part.

'The ceremony was brief and simple. About half past nine the steamers proceeded towards St. Michael's Mount, then turned and entered the harbour, cheers greeting them at the harbour mouth, but more particularly as they entered the dock. The dock heads were well occupied by spectators, who gave three hearty rounds of applause for the Mayor and Corporation (on the QUEEN OF THE BAY), three for the docks, and a similar greeting to the Trinity steamer (ALERT) and the THAMES.

Messrs. G. Bazeley and Sons' steamer the THAMES, had the honour of being the first merchant vessel to enter the docks after the formal opening; and on Tuesday, the s.s. GERVASE, belonging to the same firm, came into the docks to unload.'

Four-ship service schedule

By this time Bazeleys had given up the idea of their Liverpool service. Instead, with their four steamers PROGRES, STOCKTON, THAMES and GERVASE, they extended their London and Bristol service to a twice-weekly one in each direction. Saturdays remained their main sailing day, with the extra service setting out on Wednesdays - a vessel departing from London and Bristol on each sailing day. Along with the augmented sailing schedule, Bazeleys now advertised cabin and deck passenger fares between all their ports of call. There was an increasing call for such services, many passengers wishing to get away from the noise, dirt and rough and tumble of railway transport.

The passenger fares established at this time stood unchanged for the next 35 years, with the exception of amendments to cater for calls at Dartmouth and Plymouth as and when they were introduced.

Wreaths of smoke and clouds of bunting obscure Bazeleys' THAMES and the West Cornwall Steamship Co.'s paddle steamer QUEEN OF THE BAY, on the occasion of the opening of the New Dock at Penzance, 11th November 1884. *[Gibson & Sons]*

Bazeley's passenger fares

From	*To/from*	*Cabin*	*Return*	*Deck*	*Return*
London	Torquay	12/6d	£1/2/6d	7/6d	15/-
London	Penzance	15/-	£1/5/0	10/-	15/-
London	Bristol	£1/0/0	£1/10/0	12/6d	£1/0/0
Bristol	Penzance	10/-	£1/0/0	7/6d	15/-
Bristol	Torquay	15/-	£1/5/0	10/-	15/-
Torquay	Penzance	8/-	15/-	5/-	10/-

Working alongside their newer acquisitions, the limitations of the PROGRES became apparent: she was clearly too small and too slow. During 1884 another East Coast product was acquired to replace PROGRES, but this was no spring chicken: the Hull-registered ALBERT dating from 1856. Midway in size between the THAMES and GERVASE, in appearance she was close to the STOCKTON. Her chief attraction to Bazeleys was undoubtedly her passenger accommodation, and with double acting compound engines rated at 98 EHP, it was fully expected that she would be a fast steamer.

'Increased passenger accommodation between Penzance, London, Bristol, the s.s. ALBERT will carry between 700-800 tons, is of comparatively light draught, and has superior saloon and stateroom accommodations. She takes the place of the PROGRES, which has done good service, and is disposed of for a faster, roomier, and lighter boat.'

First noted in the Penzance shipping reports in July 1885 as under the command of Captain Spray, ALBERT's registry was not transferred to Penzance until 11th May 1886.

The PROGRES left Penzance for Bristol on the last leg of her final voyage in the London-Bristol service on 11th June 1885. Two days later she was sold out of Bazeleys' service, though they retained an 8/64ths interest. The majority 56/64ths were bought by James Henry Bennetts, a Penzance coal merchant, and she now ran as a steam collier in the West of England coastal trade. In Bennetts' service she continued to act as Bazeleys' relief vessel on occasions, but was essentially an out and out collier. Taking 1888 as a typical year, in addition to service as relief vessel on the Penzance-Scilly run in March, she made 34 round voyages between West Cornwall and South Wales or Irish Sea ports.

The ALPHA was also disposed of in 1885, being sold to the three Norman brothers of Watchet during September and October. During her final nine-month spell in Bazeleys' service she made ten round voyages (mostly between Penzance and Cardiff), bringing down 1,600 tons of coal, and carrying up 3,020 quarters of flour and 315 tons of macadam.

BETA continued in Bazeleys' ownership, though command of her now passed to Captain Mabbott of Newport. And, while her trading pattern in recent years had been quite erratic, she now picked up the ALPHA's Penzance-Cardiff trade, in which she made 18 round voyages during 1886. She was clearly a sturdy vessel. After all her earlier mishaps, she survived another major collision in August 1883, and yet another in November 1885.

The waters off Cardiff were particularly hazardous. At the time of the 1883 incident she was bound from Cardiff for Devonport with coals. Shortly after midnight on a foggy night with a light west south west wind, the steamer PETER GRAHAM (823/1873) ran into her. The steamer, which was bound from Swansea to Valencia, first sighted the BETA only 100 yards off in the fog. According to the report the 'jibboom of the schooner struck the starboard bow of the steamer,' rather than the steamer struck the schooner! But, entangled there was some bruising damage as the two vessels rolled against each other. Both vessels sustained injuries, but the BETA also lost her bowsprit and foremast. At daylight the steamer took her in tow to the Mumbles, where they left her at anchor to make repairs and work into port.

Subsequently the owners of the PETER GRAHAM sued Bazeleys for towage fees. At the hearing these were disallowed, but the master of the BETA was held to blame for the collision as he 'had his vessel under too heavy a press of canvas,' and there was no evidence that he was sounding a foghorn every two minutes as required by law.

Then on 11th November 1885 BETA collided with the Italian barque CARMANA, off Cardiff, again carrying away her bowsprit, together with two topsail yards and a cathead. She was obliged to put back to West Dock to repair.

George Bazeley died on Saturday 28th November 1886, leaving the firm in the capable hands of his two elder sons, George Paulle and William James - their younger brother Sidney Godolphin joining them within a few years.

For the next four years the firm enjoyed a prosperous period of stability with their four steamers maintaining their schedules and building their reputation for reliability. These steamers under the cloak of 'general cargo' carried an almost infinite range of commodities. Amongst these were Cornish produce in their seasons,

GERVASE working cargo alongside the Extension Pier at Penzance about 1890. Her tall funnel has now been reduced in height.

The low rail along the edge of the quay was to prevent mooring lines catching between the granite sets of the quay. Though the rail was later cut away the base of the mounts remain to this day. *[Author's collection]*

including fresh fish in the form of spring mackerel. Although highly perishable, mackerel were successfully conveyed from Penzance to London in competition with the Great Western Railway, and special facilities were laid on to convey them on to Billingsgate. Typically, during the second week in May 1888 the THAMES left Newlyn with 1,123 closed baskets, or pads, of mackerel at 2.00am on the Sunday morning, and commenced landing them in London at 12.30 on the Monday night. The mackerel (about 28 tons) were landed in good condition, and had been carried at a freight of 10d. per pad - against the 3s per pad normally charged by the railway company Several other consignments were shipped away during the following week, with the STOCKTON taking 1,500 pads and the ALBERT a similar quantity. New potatoes were also carried, but there was great competition for this trade, and Bazeleys' steamers usually carried only small quantities of 40 tons or less to Bristol.

Troubled times

The arrival of the 1890s marked the opening of a troubled period. At first there was some good fortune, when in January 1890 the GERVASE picked up a useful salvage tow. Off Portland she fell in with the derelict Norwegian barque HARMONIE (406/1873) of Arendal, laden with Norwegian timber for Cape Town. After two attempts a line was successfully passed and she was towed into Portland Road. But May saw a reversal of fortune. Just after rounding the Land's End for Bristol, the ALBERT broke her main shaft, but was able to limp back to Penzance under her own power. Worse was to follow for on 28th June Bazeleys suffered their first loss. The old schooner BETA was in collision just once too often. Again just off Cardiff, she was run down by an unidentified steamer and sank. Fortunately, Captain Mabbott and his crew were all able to get away in their boat, and reached shore safely.

If 1890 saw a turn for the worse, 1891 continued the trend. The THAMES drove ashore in thick fog on the Chesil Bank near Portland on 2nd January. Holed in the bows, the fore compartment was open to the sea, but the bulkheads held. Even so, despite valiant efforts by Captain Tom Beckerleg and his crew, assisted by local coastguards and men under Mr. Batt, the Lloyd's Agent at Weymouth, she remained fast. Much of her cargo of macadam was discharged over the side, and only the consignments of tin ingots were saved. Two tugs - Cosens' QUEEN (146/1883), and Watkins' OCEANA (337/1889) - stood by to try and tow her off the beach, but Captain Beckerleg was afraid she would founder in deep water, and that attempt was abandoned. She quickly became a constructive total loss.

Then, just six months later, fire broke out in the ALBERT's stern - by coincidence quite near to the place where the THAMES had driven ashore. She had left London for Torquay, Penzance and Bristol on the Wednesday night, and the fire broke out during her passage down Channel. Though confined to the afterpart of the vessel, the engine room had to be abandoned and with steam exhausted she lay stopped in the water for some time before HMS CALYPSO arrived. CALYPSO towed her into Weymouth, but the engineroom was almost completely gutted. Bazeleys were reluctant to spend any money on this old vessel and negotiated her sale to their friend John Williams of Penzance and Liverpool, a trader in vegetable produce. After lying a couple of months at Weymouth, and still under Bazeleys' flag, she was put under the command of Captain Nicholas Jaco for passage to Liverpool under tow. Within six months Bazeleys had lost half of their steam fleet, though it would appear that they were adequately insured.

MERCUTIO off Hotwells waiting to enter the floating harbour about 1890. Note the lighthouse on the forecastle head for the navigation light: see *Record* 8, pages 250-251 for correspondence on this subject. The foreshortening effect of the bows-on angle gives her a stubby appearance. The vessel astern looks like the CLOCH, but it was unusual for two of Bazeleys' vessels to arrive on the same day, let alone the same tide.*[Bristol City Museum, York collection P.3984M]*

CLOCH passing under the Clifton Suspension Bridge on her way down from Bristol docks about 1895. She still sports her original tall funnel, the upper section of which was later removed. *[Bristol City Museum, York collection P.3980M]*

The loss of the THAMES was quickly made good by the purchase of the MERCUTIO. A fine coastal steamer, after the style of the GERVASE but larger, she was a valuable addition to their stock. Of similar profile to the GERVASE, with a well deck forward, engines amidships with a long raised quarterdeck and deck cranes, she had two clearly distinguishing features. One either side of her forecastle, sailing ship fashion, she sported white lighthouses carrying her port and starboard sidelights. Completed at Dalmuir in 1879, she could carry 1,150 tons of bulk cargo. Her registration was transferred to Penzance on 30th September1891, when the three Bazeley brothers were registered as joint owners. Like the GERVASE, the MERCUTIO proved an excellent workhorse, and served the firm till the end of their trading days. Initially both the GERVASE and MERCUTIO had very tall funnels, in the case of the former to the height of her mast hounds. These created excessive draft and heavy fuel consumption and were in due course reduced to a more economic working height.

Replacing the ALBERT took a little longer, but within five months of the accident, and two months of her subsequent disposal, Bazeleys acquired the SHAMROCK. She was a little smaller than the MERCUTIO, and was possibly not so well adapted for this service. No pictures of her have yet come to light. Her registration was transferred to Penzance on 9th October 1891.

Captain Hodge now had the MERCUTIO; Captain Spray the GERVASE; Captain Jaco the SHAMROCK; and Captain Edwards the STOCKTON. In this allocation of commands tons burthen was the deciding factor in determining the pecking order. One consequence of the move to larger vessels was an increased consumption of fuel. A larger craft than the little QUEEN was now required to meet their needs, and of course the BETA had also been lost so they had no reserve capacity. In April 1892, the Dutch-built schooner EUGENIE AUGUSTE was bought to take on these duties. At first under the command of James Rowe she made twenty-three voyages between Newport and Bristol in 1893. The QUEEN had been extensively employed between Cardiff and Bristol. But in the second half of 1886, in addition to thirteen such voyages, she also made one to Torquay with coal, and nine between Torquay and Dartmouth with general cargo - when no doubt acting as a local feeder and distributor for their Torquay service. With the acquisition of the EUGENIE AUGUSTE the QUEEN was not disposed of, but became more or less a hulk in Bristol floating harbour. Even so her registration as a British vessel was maintained until 1906, in case of need, and for each half of 1894 she had a master and three ABs attached to her on pay.

Enhanced passenger facilities

In 1894 Bazeleys moved on to the next stage of developing their service, beginning to acquire vessels with improved passenger facilities. They were never in the market for new tonnage but were keen to acquire vessels with an established pedigree. The first of these was the fine coastal cargo liner CLOCH of Glasgow, which had two full decks and accommodation far superior to any vessel that had previously been employed by the Bazeleys. She was brought down from Glasgow to Bristol, and entered her new service when she sailed for Penzance and London on Saturday 19th May 1894. On her first call at Penzance the public and the press were permitted to view her splendour. The published report informed all that:

'Her saloon can with ease accommodate 33 passengers, and extra room can be found for ten more should the occasion arise. The steerage department has accommodation for 44 passengers. The saloon is a beautiful compartment and is fitted in rosewood, maple and oak with a ceiling of white and gold. Separate cabins are provided for ladies, with proper lavatory accommodation, and there is a cosy smoking saloon on deck.'

Her compound engines were capable of driving the ship at over 10 knots. With engines amidships, most of the stern of the steamer was given over to accommodation, though there was a small aft hold between the engineroom and the accommodation. She was able to carry a useful 800 tons of cargo in addition to her complement of passengers. CLOCH now set the standard, serving as a bench mark for all future Bazeley acquisitions.

But, despite a more modern fleet of superior vessels, accidents continued to occur. During March 1893 the MERCUTIO collided with Coppack's Chester schooner JAMES RENNIE (204/1876). Running on to her in thick fog off Dover the steamer sliced into the schooner, and she sank in eight minutes. The MERCUTIO was brought round and picked up her crew of seven, landing them in Dover.

Twelve months later the MERCUTIO was again in trouble, this time on the River Avon in a potentially much more serious incident. On the night of Saturday 16th March 1894, under the command of Captain Spray, but in the charge of a pilot, she was going down the Avon when she struck a glancing blow on a rock. Her bow was opened up well below the water line and her fore-bulkhead breached. She began to settle quickly by the head, and by the time she was run onto the muddy bank, to prevent her sinking in the fairway, the water was up to her 'tween-deck beams. As a further complication, water getting into some lime casks started a fire, but this was quickly got under control. A temporary patch was fitted with the aid of the Corporation dredger alongside pumping, and the next tide she was got off, taken down to Avonmouth to turn, and brought back to Bristol. Her cargo was later transferred to the SHAMROCK before she was taken into dry dock on the 19th for the damage to be made good.

The old STOCKTON was now the weak link in Bazeleys' four ship service. Over thirty years old she had considerably less freeboard and less carrying capacity than any of the others. This lack of freeboard no doubt contributed to the loss of her mate, James Joyce, when he disappeared overboard off Dartmouth in November 1893.

Although the STOCKTON had been clearly recognised as the weakest element of the little fleet, another four years were to pass before her disposal was negotiated. Before this occurred she too was involved in a collision on the Thames. In May 1896 while running down the Thames, the STOCKTON collided with and sank the ANN WEBSTER (792/1870). At the subsequent Admiralty hearing Bazeleys admitted liability but asked for this to be limited to the £8 per ton prescribed by the Merchant Shipping Act, and this was agreed.

No clear reason has been identified as to why STOCKTON was kept for so long. It may in part have been due to some apprehensions about the SHAMROCK, and in part because there were no suitable vessels on the market. However, in April 1897 it was announced that the STOCKTON had been sold to Fowey proprietors, to be replaced by the SKERRYVORE, and her registration was transferred to Fowey on 4th May. Here Toyne, Carter and Co. managed her for many years, in the china clay trade, before she was sold in the early 1900s to work out of Goole. At some time her clipper bow was remodelled into a spoon, and she was fitted with three whaleback deckhouses to counter her lack of freeboard. She eventually foundered in a gale during December 1909.

Her replacement, SKERRYVORE, was also purchased from the Clyde Shipping Co., and was a fine vessel in a similar style to the CLOCH, but a little larger again. As soon as Board of Trade permission could be obtained she was renamed COATH, being registered at Penzance on 20th September 1897. Within a month of the acquisition of the COATH, Bazeleys completed the sale of the SHAMROCK to German owners.

The two workhorses of the fleet, MERCUTIO and GERVASE, continued to provide the Wednesday heavy cargo service, while the CLOCH and COATH carried the more prestigious Saturday light cargo and passenger trade. Though far from the biggest vessels working in the Bristol trade, these last two were of good size, and navigating the Avon was a tricky business for all craft. In October 1898, when dropping down from Bristol on the early afternoon tide of Saturday 8th October, the CLOCH took the ground just down river from the Clifton suspension bridge. On a dropping tide she stuck fast and developed a marked list. All efforts to float her on the next morning's tide failed. She was refloated on the Monday afternoon's tide and was towed back to the pontoon off the mouth of the Cumberland Basin. Here the work of discharging her cargo continued, and she was later allowed into the floating harbour to make full repairs.

COATH alongside Bazeleys' sheds at Beacon Quay, Torquay about 1900, still sporting the tall funnel from her Clyde days. *[World Ship Photo Library]*

Two views of CLOCH aground in the Avon between 8th-10th October 1898. Alongside to port are the tug BELLE ISLE, providing steam for the centrifugal pumps, and an old trow receiving cargo. Black smoke pours from the twin funnels of the docks' vessel on her starboard side. With CLOCH listing towards the camera, the upper shot gives a good impression of her deck arrangement. *[Bristol City Museum, York collection P.3490M and P.3500M]*

SOLWAY with a brave display of flags - including Bazeleys' houseflag at the main - passing St. Michael's Mount. *[Paul Brothers, Penzance - George Scott collection]*

George Bazeley and Sons Ltd.

In late1905 and early 1906, title in the CLOCH, COATH and MERCUTIO was transferred to George Bazeley and Sons Ltd. George Paulle Bazeley alone owned the GERVASE and she was not transferred to the new company. While she still had many years of useful work ahead of her, her facilities were inadequate to the changing needs of the company and the increasing demand of mid-week passengers. In May 1907 another Clyde steamer, the SOLWAY, replaced the GERVASE.

'Few short sea trips are more pleasant than those which are provided by the vessels of the Little Western Steamship Company, which run between London and Bristol, calling at Torquay and Penzance, and evidently the facilities which this company offer are becoming more highly appreciated the more they are known. To meet the growing demand for passenger accommodation, the company have just disposed of the GERVASE, which had been engaged in the trade between the above ports for some years and have replaced her by the SOLOWAY (sic), a larger ship of about the same dimensions as the COATH, another of the Company's steamers.

She has accommodation for 40 passengers, and this with the facilities offered by the other steamers of the same line, should go a long way to meeting the demand on the part of passengers during the holiday season. The SOLOWAY arrived at Penzance for the first time on Saturday afternoon. The GERVASE has now gone into the Portuguese wine trade.'

SOLWAY was a typical Clyde coastal liner of the period. Captain Hodge shifted his command to the new steamer, and with a crew of 16 she was licensed to carry 44 cabin passengers, with another 83 on deck. She saw her share of incidents and during her first year in Bazeleys' service she was run into on the Thames:

'Jan 23, 1908 - off Greenwich Jan 24 - Took a compulsory pilot on board off Gravesend and proceeded up river. When off Greenwich saw several steamers at anchor and also at 2.30p.m. saw a fog in Long Reach. Our engines were stopped and then put full speed astern and all way stopped on the ship, and drifting with the flood tide. The steam whistle was sounded several times, three blasts, to let the SAMUEL HOUGH know we were stopped but he came on at great speed and when about a length off my starboard quarter he went full speed astern. He came on and gave the SOLWAY a scarring blow on the starboard side amidships breaking the main rail and breaking one boat's skids and bending another and denting the half-round iron in the covering board and bending the rail and breaking the wash streak aft and denting the quarter badge piece. As soon as we could see a clear berth came to anchor. Now a dense fog.
Jacob Hodge, Master - John Sampson, Mate.'

The damage did not prevent SOLWAY sailing on schedule, and full repairs were made at Penzance during her next call.

Despite being able to carry more passengers than either the CLOCH or the COATH, the SOLWAY appears to have had some drawbacks. After she had been in Bazeleys' service for only three years, they acquired an even bigger Clyde steamer the VALENCIA, and sold the SOLWAY a year later. The VALENCIA now became the biggest steamer in Bazeleys' fleet. Again she was owned by George P. Bazeley alone for the first few months until her formal transfer to the company in the September. Then renamed CADOC, she was close to the maximum size suitable for working regularly out of Penzance. Loaded she drew nearly 17 feet of water, which was close to the maximum draft over the dock sill during neap tide periods. In March 1911, after declaring that they drew only 16 feet, she was allowed by the harbourmaster to enter dock at one and a half-hours ebb. She struck the sill, doing minimal damage but incurring the wrath of the harbour master and the censure of the Dock Committee when it was found that she in fact was drawing 16 feet 9 inches aft.

Absorbtion by Coast Lines

The ten-year period leading up to the First World War saw the West Cornwall fisheries at their lowest ebb, in so far as the local fishermen were concerned. Visiting East

Coast steam drifters had virtually driven them from the seas and to earn a living many young men then went away 'steam-boating'. Today old men, several recall leaving Penzance virtually penniless and remember with thanks the blind eye turned when they hopped aboard one of the Bazeley boats for a free passage to Bristol - being just expected to help out on deck. From Bristol they spent what little they had catching a train over to Cardiff, where they tramped the streets of Tiger Bay and dossed wherever they could until they got a berth and shipped out foreign.

At Bristol the EUGENIE AUGUSTE was sold to Thomas Robert Brown, lightermen in February 1902, and the QUEEN was sold for breaking in January 1906. The price of steam coal at Bristol must now have been sufficiently competitive to outweigh the cost of running their own bunker service.

During the First World War, Bazeley's only loss was the COATH. She was listed as missing since 13th December 1916, and Bazeleys were advised by the Admiralty that she must be given up as a total loss. In fact, she had sunk with all hands after being torpedoed off Beachy Head on 12th December. CADOC, CLOCH and MERCUTIO now maintained the London-Bristol service, but the end of the little company was in sight.

The expansion of Coast Lines Ltd. was well under way, with its planned assimilation of established companies. Detailed facts relating to the end of the Little Western Steamship Co. are hard to find. The three surviving vessels continued to trade until 1920, and local tradition has it that Bazeleys continued to trade profitably during this period. Early in 1920 they were bought out by the expanding Coast Lines Ltd. - supposedly at the top of the market. Coast Lines' chairman reported to his board on 10th February that 'negotiations had been entered into with the Little Western Steamship Company of Bristol for the purchase of their steamers, trade and assets, for the sum of £160,000.' Assuming that this was close to the sum paid - and the rapid conclusion of the deal would support this - it was a very good price as far as the Bazeleys were concerned. The three steamers can not have been worth much more than £45,000, so allowing over £100,000 for the assets and goodwill, this was indeed an opportune sale for the Bazeley brothers.

Coast Lines took over the running of their ships in the spring of 1920, the CLOCH being recorded as sold to them on 3rd March, with the CADOC and MERCUTIO following the next day. With their acquisition the Little Western Steamship Company now came under Coast Lines management, and its registered office was removed to London. In December this operating company was put into voluntary liquidation and wound up. After a little over forty years of very successful trading, Bazeleys and Sons of Penzance and their Little Western Steamship Company ceased to exist.

It is quite apparent that there was only a secondary interest in acquiring their steamers. Coast Lines' principal objective was to acquire the trade of the company, eliminating their competition. CLOCH was immediately sold off, but CADOC and MERCUTIO continued in Coast Lines' service for several years, the latter retaining her original name and Penzance registration. CADOC, however, was transferred to Liverpool and renamed NORFOLK COAST to replace one of Coast Lines early losses.

[Bazeleys' fleet list, with further photographs, will appear in *Record* 12.]

From a cracked and damaged negative, this view of CADOC is far from perfect, yet is significant for being the only shot so far found of the ship, and for showing her in First World War camouflage paint. After Coast Lines Ltd. took over Bazeleys' services and fleet, she served for a dozen years as NORFOLK COAST, but still managed to elude the camera.

PILGRIM SHIP FOLLOW-UP

THE END OF A PILGRIM SHIP - SUNK BY A 'K'CLASS SUBMARINE

Richard Cornish

H.M. Ships usually only get the briefest of mentions in *Record* but in this instance a little more is warranted. It could be said the story starts in 1899 with the building of the ship BOSNIA (7,436/1899) for HAPAG in Palmer's yard at Newcastle-upon-Tyne. She commenced her working life in the North Atlantic passenger cargo service but in 1907 was converted by Blohm und Voss into an emigrant ship. This involved some changes to her outward appearance, the most obvious being the exchange of her four raking masts for two almost vertical ones and a funnel to match. She remained with her owners until 1920 when she was handed over to Great Britain as part of the First World War reparations, the Shipping Controller appointing McVicar, Marshall and Co. Ltd as her managers.

In 1922 she was purchased by Hajee M.H. Namazee of Hong Kong to operate on the Indonesia-Jeddah pilgrim route and was renamed FRANGESTAN, by now her gross tonnage had increased to 9,683. She formed part of a small fleet of second-, third- or even fourth-hand ships assembled by Hajee Namazee to operate in the lucrative pilgrim trade. FRANGESTAN, despite her conversion, still retained her first class passenger accommodation as well as considerable cargo carrying capacity. On 2nd April 1924 she came into the news. She was on passage from Bombay bound for Genoa and Barcelona via Jeddah carrying a full cargo, 15 European passengers, 1,221 pilgrims and a crew of 140 when at 07.00 it was discovered that the cotton loaded in No. 2 hold 'tween deck was on fire. Cotton is notorious for the intensity of the heat produced when it burns and it is very difficult to extinguish. This soon proved to be the case as the succession of radio message reports in *Lloyd's List* for that date indicates. In all no less than 47 ships acknowledged receipt of her distress signals and many of them altered course to proceed to her assistance.

The first to arrive on the scene was the Clan Line steamer CLAN MACIVER, (4,606/1921), under the command of Captain A.D. Turton. Soon after her arrival the Master of the burning FRANGESTAN decided to transfer his passengers and this was achieved with the four lifeboats from the Clan ship, but by the time it was complete the fire was really out of hand so the pilgrim ship was abandoned. The European passengers left first with all their baggage, then the pilgrims and finally the Chinese crew and British officers. The latter part of the transfer in darkness was illuminated by searchlight from an Italian passenger ship which also served to show the large number of sharks hopefully following each of the boats. A Reuters' report of an interview with passenger Sir Derrick Watson appeared in *Lloyd's List* of 5th April. It quotes 'an old bearded pilgrim offered his small vessel of holy water in a last effort to quell the furnace' and 'As the Captain of the FRANGESTAN left his ship he paused on the gangway to light a cigarette, and simultaneously the gangway itself took fire' - not exactly in the usual style of Lloyd's factual casualty reporting!

The photograph of the FRANGESTAN sinking by the stern (above) appeared in the *Illustrated London News* for 17th May 1924.

She is seen left in earlier life with her original four masts as HAPAG's BOSNIA. *[Peter Newall collection]*

At 21 00 local time another Hajee Namazee ship arrived on the scene, the clipper-stemmed, ex-Ben Line ship BENCLEUCH, now renamed TANGISTAN, and she followed the CLAN MACIVER into Port Sudan. There the pilgrims were transferred to the Hajee ship for the last leg of their journey to Jeddah on the opposite side of the Red Sea whilst the Clan ship carried on to Suez. Meanwhile H.M. Submarine K26, almost brand new and on her way out east, came upon the still floating, burning hulk of the FRANGESTAN. Her Captain, Commander G.P. Thomson OBE RN, was asked to evaluate the possibility of salvage but he rated this as nil, the fire preventing anyone boarding her. As by then she was a danger to navigation he was ordered to sink her. This was carried out on the morning of 4th April and is recorded by a few laconic entries in her log for that day as follows: '0935: Proceeded to get into position for firing at FRANGESTAN. 0955: Commenced firing at FRANGESTAN with No.3 gun at 200X with HE and practice. 1115: Finished firing (50 rounds used). 1145: Stopped both. 1321: FRANGESTAN sunk in pos. 19° 53N 39° 35°E. 1330: proc. course 151° 12 kt.'

K26, said to be the largest submarine in the world when completed, was an Improved K Class, the only one ever built and a great improvement on her seventeen predecessors of the first type. She at least sank a ship with her armament which was more than any other K Class succeeded in doing.

MORE FOR MECCA
Anthony Cooke

I greatly enjoyed Peter Newall's interesting article 'Pilgrim ships for Mecca' in *Record* 9. Given the constraints of space he could hardly cover all the hundreds of ships which have carried Mohammedan pilgrims over the years, but it may be worth adding just a few more names.

Before the closure of the Suez Canal in 1967 the quotas of pilgrims from North and West Africa were carried by sea. In those final years the contract to transport the Libyan contingent was held by the Greek shipping tycoon John Latsis whose vessels also carried pilgrims on occasion from Morocco, Algeria, Senegal, Lebanon and Indonesia. For this purpose he bought a number of quite large and well-known liners.

In 1959 he acquired two of the ex-Nelson Line motorships from Royal Mail Lines, the HIGHLAND BRIGADE (14,216/1929) which he renamed HENRIETTA (later MARIANNA), and the HIGHLAND PRINCESS (14,216/1930) which he called MARIANNA. His announced intention was to run the pair in the still-booming migrant trade to Australia. In fact, this plan was abandoned and the ex-HIGHLAND PRINCESS was sold. Her sister, however, was rebuilt as a pilgrim-carrier, losing her two stump funnels in the process and acquiring a single more modern one.

In 1963 Mr. Latsis bought two converted Victory ships, the GROOTE BEER (9,140/1944) which became the MARIANNA IV, and the WATERMAN (9,124/1945) which he called MARGARITA. They had hitherto been mainly used as Dutch Government emigrant ships. In the same year he made his biggest passenger ship purchases, the well-known P&O mailships STRATHMORE (23,580/1935) and STRATHEDEN (23,732/1937). These became the MARIANNA LATSI and the HENRIETTA LATSI, but later swapped names. They were almost certainly the biggest ships ever used in regular pilgrim service. Once the brief annual pilgrim season was over, most of these Latsis vessels would be laid up - they can hardly have been profitable but were perhaps intended more to establish their owner's pro-Arab credentials at a time when he was moving into the oil-refining business and to help cement his relations with the Saudi Royal Family.

As mentioned in Peter Newall's article, the China Navigation Company took over the Malaysian

MARIANNA, ex HIGHLAND BRIGADE, as rebuilt by John Latsis with one funnel. She was broken up in Taiwan in 1965. *[A. Duncan courtesy World Ship Photo Library collection]*

KING ABDELAZIZ had a remarkable string of former names. Beginning life as MISSOURIAN for the American-Hawaian Steamship Co., she was acquired as part of a job lot of ageing US tonnage by the Ministry of Shipping in 1940 and became EMPIRE SWAN, although within two years she was placed under the control of the exiled Government of Belgium as BELGIAN FREIGHTER. After the war she became the CAPITAINE POTIE of Compagnie Maritime Belge, but was sold to Italy in 1948 as GENOVA. In 1955 a heroic reconstruction saw her emerge as FLAMINIA, with a passenger capacity put at 1,024, presumably for the emigrant trade. The name KING ABDELAZIZ was bestowed on her by Bakhashab Mohamed Abubakur in 1964 when she came under Saudi Arabian ownership, carrying pilgrims to Jeddah for a few years. She was sold to Italian breakers in 1968, but the deal must have fallen through, or she was resold, and she finally went to Kaohsiung for demolition, arriving in April 1970. *[World Ship Photo Library collection]*

pilgrim contract from Holts in 1953. Initially, the ANKING (6,127/1950) and ANSHUN (6,160/1951) assumed the Blue Funnel colours for their pilgrim voyages, presumably because Holts had been so well established in the trade. As both companies had a predilection for very tall, upright funnels the ploy may have succeeded. Like several other companies, China Navigation also sometimes took on additional charters to bring pilgrims from Aqaba, Aden or the Sudanese ports. Then, in 1958 the ANKING was chartered to the Pan-Islamic Steamship Company but the personal habits of some of the Pakistani pilgrims prompted complaints from the ship's officers. China Navigation lost the Malaysian contract to the thrusting Abeto company after 1970.

Abeto, which already had the Indonesian pilgrim contract, was a short-lived concern which briefly owned no fewer than six former French liners, ex-Messageries Maritimes, Chargeurs Reunis and Fraissinet. Two were destroyed by fire.

Some other well-known liners made at least one or two pilgrim voyages in the post-war years, including British India's KARANJA (carrying South African Mohammedans), Chandris's CHARLTON SOVEREIGN, the Turkish TRABZON, French Line's North African packets VILLE D'ALGER, and VILLE D'ORAN and the Norwegian SKAUGUM.

The Saudis themselves carried large numbers of pilgrim passengers on their regular Red Sea services. Among their more notable ships were Orri Navigation's MECCA (3,858/1950), once the Icelandic liner GULFOSS, and Saudi Lines' veteran KING ABDELAZIZ (8,779/1922) which had started her varied life as an American funnel-less motor freighter and, after much conversion, had been the Italian GENOVA and later FLAMINIA, one of the less desirable of the port-war emigrant ships.

Today, pilgrims from the more distant countries almost always make their journey of a lifetime by air, but many of the Faithful from the lands around the Red Sea still travel by ship, using the ferries which maintain regular services in the area.

British India's KARANJA (10,294/1948), seen leaving Durban in August 1974, made occasional pilgrim voyages. *[Malcolm Cranfield]*

EMPIRE FOWEY'S NEW ENGINES
Tony Smythe and John B. Hill

As Peter Newall says of SAFINA-E-HUJJAJ (ex EMPIRE FOWEY), when built as POTSDAM her machinery installation was of a somewhat revolutionary nature. Her builders, Blohm und Voss, persuaded the reluctant owners to install a highly-innovative turbo-electric propulsion plant. Not that turbo-electric machinery was unique in passenger liners - such a system had been fitted in P&O's VICEROY OF INDIA six years earlier - but the steam pressure for which the turbines were designed and the boilers were technically very advanced for their day. POTSDAM was fitted with four Benson high-pressure, forced-circulation boilers with a working pressure of 1,150 psi. The boilers provided steam to two turbines which were linked to two 10,000 kW generators operating at 3,000 rpm, driving two electric motors developing 26,000 SHP.

The boilers operated with only a small amount of water and full steam pressure could be raised in a matter of minutes. It was said that the engines could be reversed from full power ahead to full astern in 30 seconds, but this required very sophisticated controls, the boilers being particularly sensitive; the smallest error in monitoring water circulation and firing was likely to result in tube failure. Not surprisingly, such an installation required very experienced operators, and by the time the POTSDAM fell into British hands at the end of the war it was no longer possible to guarantee reliable performance. Her old chief engineer predicted that her machinery would be a big problem to his British counterpart. He was soon proved right, and following numerous problems, and after only one voyage, she was laid up.

It was concluded that only a complete set of new machinery would cure her problems. She was sent to Alexander Stephen and Sons Ltd., Glasgow, where new engines and boilers had to be designed to fit into the space available. Her boilers were replaced by Foster Wheeler-type boilers operating at 500 psi, while her turbo-electric installation was replaced by two sets of Parsons double-reduction turbines. She now developed only 18,000 SHP and her speed was reduced to about 18 knots. Her refit lasted from March 1947 to March 1950. It was the replacement of the machinery, and not the conversion into a troopship, which took so long.

EMPIRE FOWEY.

PACIFIC ABETO
John B. Hill

The illustration of the former French passenger liner BELLE ABETO brought to mind another pilgrim ship of the Arafat fleet, which seems to have gone almost unrecorded. I refer to the former Pacific Steam Navigation Company's cargo ship FLAMENCO, which was sold to the Hong Kong operator, the Ta Hing Co., in 1966, and transferred to full Arafat control in 1971.

The FLAMENCO was a product of the Greenock Dockyard Co. Ltd. in 1950. Turbine engined, with a speed of 16½ knots, she was sturdily built to Clan Line specification, which is probably why the ship fetched the very good price of £334,000 when sold at 16 years of age.

Renaming her PACIFIC ABETO, the new owners removed the ship from Lloyd's class shortly

after purchase and this is probably why no notations, or dates, relating to her conversion into a pilgrim ship appear in *Lloyd's Register.* It is not known where the ship was altered, but she entered the pilgrim business with accommodation for 1,550 passengers. Deck houses were extended aft from the midships structure, at either side of No. 4 hatch, whilst the 'tween decks were furnished to accommodate pilgrims and fitted with portholes along port and starboard sides. It appears that only one additional pair of lifeboats was added (by No. 2 hatch), but liferafts were carried on platforms, created from extended masthouses.

Painted white, with a broad green band around the hull, the PACIFIC ABETO was an attractive-looking ship, but I have only come across one photograph of her, probably an Arafat official photo, which appeared in an article by Peter T. Eisele, entitled 'Indonesian Pilgrim Ships', published in the Fall 1976 Issue of *Steamboat Bill* (Steamship Historical Society of America).

In August 1976, the PACIFIC ABETO laid up at Jakarta and, after being idle for 5 years, arrived at Chittagong on 22nd August 1981 for demolition.

No doubt there will be many readers who recall this post-war PSNC ship, but I wonder how many are aware of her subsequent career? It is almost certain the ship never re-appeared in European waters in her new guise.

John Lingwood, in his article 'The Steam Conquistadores', (*Sea Breezes* March and April 1977), does not mention the FLAMENCO's conversion and neither does Duncan Haws in his PSNC volume: is this because there are no readily available references to her becoming a pilgrim ship?

Incidentally, Peter Eisele suggests that PACIFIC ABETO was probably the only vessel to enter the pilgrim trade which was not built as a passenger ship, that is apart from some Blue Funnel and other cargo liners which were seasonally employed.

A rare photograph of PACIFIC ABETO, still recognisable from PSNC days, at Singapore in March 1976. *[Malcolm Cranfield]*

SOURCES AND ACKNOWLEDGEMENTS

Photographs are from the collection of John Clarkson unless otherwise credited. We thank all who gave permission for their photographs to be used, and are particularly grateful to David Whiteside and Tony Smith of the World Ship Photo Library; and to Peter Newall, Ivor Rooke, William Schell, George Scott and the museums and institutions listed for help in finding photographs.

In researching captions, sources have included the *Registers* of William Schell and Tony Starke, *Lloyd's Register, Lloyd's Confidential Index, Lloyd's War Losses, Mercantile Navy Lists,* and *Marine News.* Use of the facilities of the World Ship Society's Central Record, the Guildhall Library and Lloyd's Register of Shipping are gratefully acknowledged. Particular thanks also to William Schell and John Bartlett for information, to Heather Fenton for editorial work, and to Marion Clarkson for accountancy services.

The post war fleet of Alexander Shipping Co. Ltd.
Sources include *Furness Withy* by David Burrell (World Ship Society, Kendal, 1990), *Lloyd's Register,* Dennis Johnzon and personal records and recollections of the author.

Photographer in focus: Ken Cunnington
Information for the captions came from a wide variety of reference books and journals, including *DP&L* by Graeme Somner (World Ship Society, Kendal, 1995), *From America to United States,* Part Two by L.A. Sawyer and W.H. Mitchell (World Ship Society, Kendal, 1981) *Empire Ships of World War Two* by W.H. Mitchell and L.A. Sawyer (Second Edition, Lloyds of London Press, London, 1990), two articles by W.B. Hallam 'Cock Tugs of Liverpool' in *Sea Breezes* December 1963 and 'Manchester Ship Canal Tugs' in *Sea Breezes* June 1968, *Blow Five* by W.B. Hallam (JOCAST, Liverpool, 1976); *Canadian Pacific* 1883-1968 by George Musk (Canadian Pacific, 1968); History of the PZM-Group by Urbain Ureel in *Nautibel* 35 (June 1995). Thanks to Nigel Bowker for information on LANGBOURNE.

The potato ship that turned turtle
This article appeared in the 1996 edition of *Seascape,* the journal of the Friends of the Jersey Maritime Museum. The help of the Channel Islands Occupation Society (Jersey Branch) and the *Jersey Evening Post* is acknowledged.

Pilgrim ship follow-up
Richard Cornish's sources were *Lloyd's Registers, Lloyd's Lists, Sea Breezes* for May and October 1977, *The Times, Illustrated London News,* Liverpool Shipwreck and Humane Society records, PRO ADM 173, *Warships of World War 1* by H.M. Le Fleming (Ian Allan Ltd., London, 1961), *Ben Line* by Graeme Somner (World Ship Society, Kendal, 1980) and the RN Submarine Museum, Gosport.

PHOTOGRAPHER IN FOCUS: KEN CUNNINGTON

John Slavin

Ken Cunnington was born in Sheffield in 1913, but his family moved from Yorkshire to Southport in Lancashire during the First World War, reputedly because of the threat of bombing by Zeppelins. His father was in the Army at the time, serving in India and Africa, but after the war he worked for the Midland Railway at Manchester, and the family moved to Cadishead to be nearer his work.

Ken left school at 14 and became an office boy in Manchester. But after being made redundant three times by the same company, he found employment locally with Lancashire Steel at Irlam, where he worked in the Transport Department until his retirement.

He became interested in photography in the 1950s, initially taking portraits and shots of railways. His first camera was a Box Brownie, after which he used a Zeiss Ikonta and later a Ross Express, all using negatives which were 2¼" x 3 ¾". The sleeves of all his negatives were numbered with the date, speed, aperture, filters used and the angle of the sun. Ken also built his own enlarger and did all his own developing and printing.

He began ship photography because it required more sedate shutter speeds than those needed for speeding trains. Ken took most of his photographs near his home on the Manchester Ship Canal, although his favourite location was the Alfred entrance to Birkenhead Docks, where he could take photographs of ships with full funnels, as opposed to many of the larger ships on the Canal which had the upper part removed to pass beneath the bridges. The early Ian Allan ABC books used many of Ken's photographs, and he received the princely sum of 5/- (25p) for each one, plus a complimentary copy of the book.

Ken married Sheila in 1957, and she initially helped him with his developing and printing, but disapproved of his working when it was hot and sunny. Around 1960 he tapered down his photographic activities, and finally gave his negatives to local tug skipper Jim Nelson as representing part of local history. Sadly, Sheila died in 1998, but Ken retains his love of ships and railways, despite failing vision.

A selection of Ken's photographs is reproduced here by kind permission of Mrs Margaret Nelson.

EGYPTIAN PRINCE
Burntisland Shipbuilding Co. Ltd., Burntisland; 1951, 3,364gt, 364 feet
4-cyl. Doxford oil engine 2SCSA by Hawthorn, Leslie and Co. Ltd., Newcastle-upon-Tyne

EGYPTIAN PRINCE is seen outward bound at Irlam on one of her regular sailings to the Mediterranean, a service which was latterly worked in conjunction with fellow-members of the Furness Group, Manchester Liners, as the Manchester Prince Line.

EGYPTIAN PRINCE and her sister SCOTTISH PRINCE were sold in 1968, the former becoming the Cyprus-registered NIKOLAS S. She was broken up at Hong Kong in 1972.

AASE MAERSK (top)
Odense Staalskibs A/S, Odense, Denmark; 1930, 6,185gt, 424 feet
Oil engine 7-cyl. 2SCSA by Burmeister & Wain, Copenhagen, Denmark
Although tankers were - and remain - common along the Manchester Ship Canal in the 1950s, the Esso-chartered AASE MAERSK was something of a head-turner. Pastel-coloured hulls, like owner A.P. Moller's trademark light-blue, were then rare and she stood out amongst the black and grey hulls. Pronouncing her name also gave local enthusiasts some difficulty, whilst for a tanker her age was remarkable: those of her contemporaries who escaped the war having mostly been scrapped. AASE MAERSK just made it to her thirtieth birthday, arriving at Preston on 20th December 1960 to be broken up by T.W. Ward Ltd.

DAN-Y-BRYN (bottom)
Burntisland Shipbuilding Co. Ltd., Burntisland; 1940, 5,217gt, 436 feet
T. 3-cyl. by David Rowan and Co. Ltd., Glasgow
DAN-Y-BRYN was built for Ambrose, Davies and Matthews Ltd. of Swansea, but registered under a variety of company names. When photographed - despite her Welsh name (it means 'under the hill') - she was owned by United Transports Ltd. of Jersey. In 1960 she went to Hong Kong owners as OCEAN GEM, becoming TOSA BAY in 1962 and being broken up in Hong Kong in 1967. In this low-angled shot, the Manchester Ship Canal does seem to merit its nickname 'the ditch.'

RIXTON (top)
J.T. Eltringham and Co., South Shields; 1905, 158gt, 106 feet
2-cyl. by Hepple and Co., South Shields
This fine pictorial view shows the last of the MSC's celebrated paddle tugs helping the Norwegian tanker AMICA (5,010/1946) pass beneath Warburton Bridge. RIXTON was sold in 1955 and converted into a barge.

GLIWICE (bottom)
Swan, Hunter & Wigham Richardson Ltd., Newcastle-upon-Tyne; 1938, 1,446gt, 253 feet
C. 2-cyl. and low-pressure turbine by Swan, Hunter & Wigham Richardson Ltd., Newcastle-upon-Tyne
GLIWICE was built as LIDA for the Polish-British Steamship Co. Ltd. of Gdynia, a company owned 75% by the Polish Government and 25% by Ellerman's Wilson Line. In 1946 LIDA was summarily nationalised by the new Polish Government and, renamed GLIWICE in 1950, continued running to British ports, latterly for Polska Zegluga Morska of Szczecin. Laid up in 1967 she was used as a floating warehouse until broken up in 1970.

EMPRESS OF SCOTLAND (top)
Fairfield Shipbuilding and Engineering Co. Ltd., Govan; 1930, 26,313gt, 667 feet
Six steam turbines geared to two shafts by Fairfield Shipbuilding and Engineering Co. Ltd., Govan
EMPRESS OF SCOTLAND was photographed as she arrived at the Pier Head from Gladstone Dock to load passengers for another voyage to Montreal. As EMPRESS OF JAPAN she had been built for Canadian Pacific's trans-Pacific service, and was probably the best passenger vessel on the service when built. She spent the entire war trooping, and was renamed EMPRESS OF SCOTLAND in October 1942 as a result of some unpleasantness involving the husband of her original namesake.

After a prolonged refit, EMPRESS OF SCOTLAND returned to service in May 1950, this time on the North Atlantic. She was laid up at Liverpool in the winter of 1957, but found new buyers, the Hamburg-Atlantic Line, who renamed her HANSEATIC for a service from Cuxhaven to New York. This was terminated by a disatrous fire at New York in September 1966, after which she was towed back home to Hamburg to be broken up.

SCHOLAR (bottom)
New England Shipbuilding Corporation, Portland, Maine, USA; 1944, 7,274gt, 442 feet
T. 3-cyl. by Harrisburg Machinery Corporation, Harrisburg, Pennsylvania, USA
One of all too few examples of Ken's photographs of ships underway on the Mersey, SCHOLAR was one of four Liberties bought by T. and J. Harrison for their Charente Steam Ship Co. Ltd. She had been built for lend-lease to the UK as SAMIDWAY and was managed for the Ministry of War Transport by Alfred Holt - a photograph of her in a slightly war-weary state appears on page 106 of *Ships in Focus: Blue Funnel Line.* Harrisons bought her in April 1947, and after a very creditable 17 years' work she went to Greeks as KOSTANTIS YEMELOS in 1964, being broken up in Japan five years later.

AMBASSADOR (top)
William Doxford and Sons Ltd., Sunderland; 1945, 7,308gt, 443 feet
Oil engine 3-cyl. 4SCSA by William Doxford and Sons Ltd., Sunderland
Hall Brothers' AMBASSADOR was part of Doxford's enormously successful 'economy' group of tramps which, with their three-cylinder oil engines, introduced many traditional tramp owners to the cost effectiveness of the motor ship. The AMBASSADOR came to a sad end, a fate mercifully more familiar from the early years of the steam tramp than from the 1960s. On 18th February 1964, whilst on a voyage from Philadelphia to London with grain her engines failed and, at the mercy of heavy seas, her hatches were stove in. The Dutch tug ELBE (797/1959) took her in tow, but the line parted and the Newcastle tramp slipped below the Atlantic on 21st February in position 37.22 north by 48.51 west.

KING ALFRED (bottom)
Greenock Dockyard Co. Ltd., Greenock; 1941, 6,919g, 432 feet
4-cyl. 2SCSA oil engine by Barclay Curle and Co. Ltd., Glasgow
Fittingly, KING ALFRED is seen off the entrance to Alfred Dock, Birkenhead - a favourite vantage point for Ken, although this day was unusually windy - a fact he noted on the negative sleeve and which is apparent from the smoke and waves. KING ALFRED was built for the Ministry of War Transport as EMPIRE RAY, Dodd, Thomson and Co. Ltd. - King Line's managers - taking over her management in 1944 on the promise of buying her after hostilities. Purchase was concluded in September 1945, and KING ALFRED traded until November 1962 when she went for lay up on the River Blackwater. She was soon sold to breakers, and arrived at Hamburg on 16th March 1963 to be demolished by Eisen und Metall A.G.

LANGBOURNE (right)
Rennie, Forrest and Co. Ltd., Wivenhoe; 1914, 69gt, 71 feet
T. 3-cyl. by Rennie, Forrest and Co. Ltd., Wivenhoe

The Liverpool Lighterage Co. Ltd. was an amalgamation in 1896 of a number of Mersey flat and tug owners, masterminded by members of the Mack family. Its fleet decreased as lighterage work on the Mersey declined, and LANGBOURNE was one of its last three tugs, the others being the BONITA, ex TID 16, which was broken up in 1963, and the KERNE which has been preserved.

LANGBOURNE was built for the Admiralty, serving initially at Chatham Dockyard as TENACITY. In 1914 she was sold to the Port of London Authority who gave her the name LANGBOURNE, and presumably continued to use her for lighterage work. Liverpool Lighterage bought her in 1948, but did not waste money on re-registering or renaming her. She was last used in 1964, and in December of that year was stripped of mast and deck fittings at Duke's Dock. On 31st May 1965 she entered Clarence Graving Dock where she was demolished.

FIGHTING COCK (bottom)
Cammell Laird and Co. Ltd., Birkenhead; 1953, 218gt, 106 feet
T. 3-cyl. by Cammell Laird and Co. Ltd., Birkenhead

Their size and shape makes tugs highly photogenic and - given the fine weather which Ken preferred for his photography - a superb portrait could result. FIGHTING COCK was owned by North West Tugs Ltd., a company owned by shipbuilders Cammell Laird, although its tugs operated as an integral part of the fleet of Liverpool Screw Towing Co. Ltd., as well as being present at most launches from the Birkenhead shipyard. FIGHTING COCK was one of the last pair of tugs for the company to be steam powered, and she makes an interesting contrast with the first tug of the name, whose photograph by Basil Feilden appeared on the cover of *Record* 4. Note the weathervane on this shot of her leading what is believed to be a Bibby liner into Birkenhead Docks. The second FIGHTING COCK became SLOYNE in 1970 following the take over of the Cock fleet by Alexandra Towing Co. Ltd., but a year later was sold to Piraeus owners as VERNICOS NICOS. She was broken up by Vioskrap Ltd. at Piraeus in 1985.

AMERICAN BUILDER (top)
Moore Dry Dock Co., Oakland, California, USA; 1945, 8,330gt, 460 feet
Two steam turbines geared to a single shaft, by the General Electric Co., Lynn, Massachusetts, USA
Unusually, Ken took this photograph from Cadishead viaduct, with a decidedy industrial background. It does show why he liked taking photographs in the Mersey as a change from his beloved Canal: the removal of the high funnel of the AMERICAN BUILDER leaves her looking decidely incomplete.

AMERICAN BUILDER was one of a group of C2-types which maintained a service from US East Coast ports to Europe. These ships, designed before the Second World War, were some of the few US-standard ships to be given melifluous names, most being called after the softwood clippers of the golden age of US shipbuilding, WHIRLWIND being the name chosen for this example. It has never been completely clear to the writer whether these ships were actually owned by their nominal operator, United States Lines, because when this company finished with AMERICAN BUILDER in 1962 she went into the US Government's reserve fleet at Suisun Bay. After eleven years there she was sold to Taiwanese breakers and demolished at Kaohsiung.

STAR OF SUEZ (bottom)
C.R.D. Adriatico, Trieste, Italy; 1948, 6,240gt, 408 feet
6-cyl. 2SCSA oil engine by C.R.D. Adriatico, Trieste, Italy
Leaving Irlam on 11th March 1954 is an Egyptian visitor to the Canal, owned by the Alexandria Navigation Co. SAE. In 1959 nationalisation of Egyptian shipping saw the STAR OF SUEZ pass to The Egyptian Navigation Co., and she continued in their ownership until sold to Brodospas, who began demolishing her at Split on 10th August 1980.

FLACHSEE (top)
Atlas-Werke A.G., Bremen, Germany; 1940, 1,335gt, 251 feet
Two 8-cyl. 4SCSA oil engines by Masch. Augsburg-Nürnberg, Augsburg, Germany
FLACHSEE had a rather exciting life. She was built for DG Neptun, Bremen as FLORA, but soon found herself in service with the Kriegsmarine in a variety of roles - a prison ship, and later as a Sperrbrecher - literally, a 'barrier breaker', and presumably intended to clear mines. In this rather dangerous role she survived until scuttled off St. Nazaire on 25th August 1944. The French salvaged her after the war, and in 1947 she went back into service as PORT NAVALO. In 1955 W. Schuchmann Reederei of Bremerhaven bought her and bestowed the name FLACHSEE. The company was associated with Bugsier, and FLACHSEE ran on their liner service to UK and Irish ports including the Mersey and Manchester. On 11th February 1963 she was bound from Cork to Bremen with general cargo when she collided with the Nassau-registered steamer CANUK TRADER (7,151/1944) in the Dover Straits and sank.

GOOTE (bottom)
T. van Duivendijk's Sch., Lekkerkerk, Netherlands; 1952, 490gt, 219 feet
8-cyl. 4SCSA oil engine by N.V. Werkspoor, Amsterdam, Netherlands
Ken took relatively few photographs of Dutch coasters, seemingly preferring to use his film on bigger, and British, ships. One of the few examples of his work showing the Dutch coaster which was reasserting its dominance of European coastal trades in the 1950s is the GOOTE, owned by P.A. Van Es & Co. N.V. Her four derricks suggests GOOTE was intended for liner trading rather than tramping.

In 1965, GOOTE was sold to Norwegian owners and renamed PERRY, and in 1972 went out to Indonesia, the last resting place of many Dutch-built coasters, as DEEPA JAYA. In 1983 *Lloyd's Register* deleted her after she had been reported broken up.

PLADDA (top)
Caledon Shipbuilding and Engineering Co. Ltd., Dundee; 1950, 854gt, 219 feet
7-cyl. 2SCSA oil engine by British Polar Engines Ltd., Glasgow
As befitted one of the world's oldest shipping companies, Clyde Shipping Co. Ltd. had a very distinctive and pleasing style for its ships, which it retained through the steam era into its final motor ship days. Calls by the company at Manchester seem to have ceased in the 1950s, but PLADDA still served Liverpool until 1963 when she was sold. This stern shot is an excellent example of the sort of intimate portrait of a ship which characterises Ken's photography on the Ship Canal.

After her sale, the PLADDA went east, and for the next twenty years carried a bewildering variety of names which disguised the fact that she had just one basic owner over this period: Guan Guan Shipping Ltd. of Singapore: RADJA MAS, CHOPIN (twice), AKASSA, KING FISH, KIM GUAN and finally KING LUCK, as which she was broken up in July 1983.

VARDAL (bottom)
Helsingörs Jernsk. & Msk., Helsingörs, Denmark; 1921, 1,546gt, 263 feet
T. 3-cyl. by Helsingörs Jernsk. & Msk., Helsingörs, Denmark
Ken photographed a number of the fascinating Scandinavian timber ships that still came to Manchester in some numbers during the fifties and sixties, and this representative is VARDAL owned by Egil Næsheim A/S of Haugesund. Well into her fourth decade when photographed, the steamer had been built as GULFAXE, had then run as POLLUX until taking the name VARDAL in 1948. The Norwegian owners sold her in favour of a motorship in 1965, and she went to Philippines owners who named her first PATRIOT and in 1967 SAN AGUSTIN. Her fate is slightly mysterious: *Lloyd's Confidential Index* reports that she was taken over by Sun Builders, Brunei in 1968, and that her present wherabouts was unknown. After 47 years, it seems most likely that the steamer was broken up.

This photograph appeared in the first edition of Ian Allan's *ABC Foreign Coastal Freighters,* where it was wrongly attributed to George Osbon.

DOTTEREL (top)
Caledon Shipbuilding and Engineering Co. Ltd., Dundee; 1934, 1,494gt, 294 feet
T. 3-cyl. by A. Stephen and Sons Ltd., Glasgow
Writing these captions has served to remind your editor, who grew up near the Manchester Ship Canal, just what a variety of ships could be seen on the Canal in the 1950s. These included some of the last steam reciprocating cargo liners, those owned by the British and Continental Steam Ship Co. Ltd. and running a service to near-European ports. DOTTEREL had joined this fleet in 1948, having been built as DUNDEE for the Dundee, Perth and London Shipping Co. Ltd., and seeing wartime service as a convoy rescue ship. In 1961 DOTTEREL was sold to Spanish breakers and demolished at Bilbao.

PACIFIC STRONGHOLD (bottom)
Vickers-Armstrongs (Ship Builders) Ltd., Newcastle-upon-Tyne; 1958, 9,439gt, 501 feet
Two steam turbines double-reduction geared to a single shaft by Parsons Marine Turbine Co., Wallsend-on-Tyne
Ken's note on the sleeve of this negative that PACIFIC STRONGHOLD was heading up the canal to load for her maiden voyage dates the shot to July or August 1958. The PACIFIC fleet of Furness, Withy and Co. Ltd. were very familiar on the Canal in the fifties and sixties, six ships the initial letters of whose second names spelt out F-U-R-N-E-S.

After a short spell in the ownership of Royal Mail Lines, PACIFIC STRONGHOLD was sold in 1971 to become AEGIS HONOR in the Papalios fleet. But sophisticated and expensive-to-run turbine ships did not often last long under flag-of-convenience ownership, and she was sold to Chinese shipbreakers in 1974.

MANCUNIUM (top)
Ferguson Brothers (Port Glasgow) Ltd., Port Glasgow; 1946, 1,334gt, 263 feet
T. 6-cyl. by Ferguson Brothers (Port Glasgow) Ltd., Port Glasgow
An extremely familiar sight in the Ship Canal for almost forty years was this twin screw sludge ship owned by, to give them their full title, the Lord Mayor, Aldermen and Citizens of the City of Manchester (Rivers Department). Seen here in original condition, in September 1962 MANCUNIUM was given twin diesels and her superstructure - but not her rather anachronistic hull - was rebuilt in a 1960s style that made her look rather ridiculous. Manchester's sewage system was taken over by the North West Water Authority in the 1970s, but MANCUNIUM continued to carry treated waste from Davyhulme Sewage Works out into the Irish Sea until 1985. She was then bought by Macclesfield-based Effluents Services Ltd., and was transferred to work in the Solent, still dumping unwanted materials at sea. After a long if unromantic career, MANCUNIUM was demolished at Newport, Gwent in March 1990.

WAYNEGATE (bottom)
Bartram and Sons Ltd., Sunderland; 1944/1948, 7,349gt, 448 feet
T. 3-cyl. by Duncan Stewart and Co. Ltd., Glasgow
This photograph shows to good effect the transom stern which distinguished the prefabricated C and D type standard ships of the Second World War. However, WAYNEGATE was not quite typical of this group although she had been laid down as the C type EMPIRE PENANG. She was completed as the maintenance ship HMS MULLION COVE and is reported to have been used for submarine repairs in the far east. In 1948 she was converted to a cargo ship, becoming the MARGARET CLUNIES for three years until Turnbull, Scott and Co. Ltd. bought her to become their second WAYNEGATE. In 1961 she was sold, and became first the Panamanian KATINGO, later the Philippine-owned PRESIDENT MAGSAYSAY and finally just MAGSAYSAY. An engine room fire off Korea on 30th July 1968 led to her abandonment, but she was reboarded, the fire put out, and towed to Pusan where she was sold to breakers in December 1968.

DOM PEDRO

Charles Dawson

Edward Paget-Tomlinson's article on Barrow-in-Furness in *Record* 6 made passing reference to DOM PEDRO. The vicissitudes of the shipping business gave her an interesting and long life, which began under the ownership of the predecessors of the Anchor Line. They were Nicol and Robert Handyside, two brothers who established themselves in Glasgow in 1838 as shipbrokers and merchants, using chartered tonnage with which to trade to the Baltic and Russia. Their family connections with Russia were very close and strong: their brother William had gone there as a young man to help his uncle Charles Baird who built Russia's first steamboat ELIZABETH, founded an engineering company in St Petersburg, and built much of the metalwork for Isaks Cathedral there. During the dozen or so years of the active Russian period of Nicol and Robert's business, Nicol was at one time Russian Vice-Consul in Glasgow.

In 1852 the firm changed its name to Handysides and Company when Captain Thomas Henderson joined them. He had been master of the paddle steamer ORION, built in 1846 by Caird and Company, Greenock for the Burns-owned Glasgow and Liverpool Steam Shipping Company, when she was wrecked off Port Patrick in June 1850 with the loss of 41 lives on her way to Liverpool. The second mate, who had been on duty on the bridge at the time of the tragedy, was deported for seven years for his gross negligence. The master, blameless though he was, fell under a cloud, and so perhaps decided that now was the time for him to change course.

Glasgow and Portugal

In 1852 the trio were bent on expanding their business. The first phase was to actually own ships, and in 1854 they started with sailing ships and with a variety of destinations including Australia and India. In 1854 N. and R. Handyside and Company, as they were now called, expanded their interests to Portugal, becoming managers of the two ships of the Glasgow and Lisbon Steam Packet Company (G&LSPC). Both ships had historic Portuguese names: VASCO DA GAMA and IGNEZ DE CASTRO. The writer's great grandfather, a Scot by the name of William Kennedy from Greenock on the River Clyde, was in command of the latter, his first steamship, when he unfortunately wrecked her off the coast of Portugal on 5th February 1859.

The first Anchor Line notice seems to have appeared in the *Glasgow Herald* of 1st May 1856 advertising the start of their Glasgow-New York service. It was also in that year that two more steamers were ordered for G&LSPC: DOM AFFONSO and DOM PEDRO. The latter was a single-screw steamer with three-masted schooner rig built of iron by Robert Steele and Company of Greenock, and appears in *Lloyd's Register* of 1860 as of 299/244 tons, with five bulkheads. Her dimensions were 159.7 x 20.1 x 12.5 feet. In 1860 her single-cylinder engine was doubled and a larger boiler installed. Captain Kennedy became her master on the Glasgow-Lisbon service during the years 1859-60 and she continued on this route until she was sold, first to Robert Little of Greenock and then to James Little in Barrow in the arrangement with Anchor Line which is described below.

DOM PEDRO, painted with all sails set. *[Charles Dawson collection]*

A number of factors led to these changes for DOM PEDRO. Railway lines were one of the products of the ironworks at Hindpool, and one of the particular customers for these sections was the Pennsylvania Railroad Company in the United States. The up-swing in trade following the depredations of the American Civil War increased demand for the company's expanding network, and the Pennsylvania Railroad Company saw a way to augment their own passenger and goods traffic by gaining control of the shipping of the material and integrating this with their own railroad system. In 1870 they had discussions with Anchor Line, ostensibly regarding making Philadelphia their US terminal. But this really seems to have been a veiled attempt to acquire the by now thriving Scottish shipping line. Anchor Line were, of course, reluctant to let the direction of their affairs be transferred completely to the American side, and rejected the approach. Pennsylvania Railroad Company riposted by providing considerable financial help in the formation of the American Steamship Company. Anchor Line were to open their own New York office in 1872.

It was at this stage that the Duke of Devonshire entered into discussions with Anchor Line, the outcome being the formation of the Barrow Steamship Company Ltd., with an authorised capital of £1 million in shares of £25 each. Among the subscribers were the Duke, with £100,000, and the two Handyside brothers with a similar sum between them. The brothers, who were by this time the principals of Anchor Line, made one stipulation: their money was to be used for ships, not docks, and the Barrow Shipbuilding Company naturally fitted into the scheme of things, and began building for Anchor Line.

Glasgow to New York

Development of the port, which included necessary dredging to permit the movement of larger ships, took longer than expected, and so, in the meantime, ANCHORIA (1) (4,157/1874) and her sisters sailed from Glasgow. To compensate for the delay in starting direct sailings from Barrow, the Anchor Line helped temporarily with the supply of coastal vessels for transhipment between Barrow and Glasgow. It was this that led to the acquisition of DOM PEDRO by James Little at Barrow: she was to be used mainly for the transhipment of luggage between the two ports. For this role she was considerably altered as can be seen from the photograph which shows her after 1872, when she was renamed ARIADNE, and with only two plain masts.

Delays to the Barrow-New York service were also aggravated by the international financial situation. The short-lived boom which succeeded the Franco-Prussian War of 1870 had already passed its peak, and by 1874 a serious recession had set in. This situation was not improved by the additional competition from a number of new US shipping lines which had been set up at the height of the boom. Besides the American Steamship Company mentioned earlier, there were the State Line and the Red Star Line. Surplus capacity meant that even the prestigious Cunard Line was forced to withdraw some of its services.

It was not until May 1880, some eight years after the inception of the idea, that Anchor Line's Barrow-New York service was inaugurated by CASTALIA (1) (2,201/1872) built by Charles Connell, Glasgow. There was, however, a poor response from the public. In an effort to stimulate more business a call at Dublin was introduced in 1881, but this was abandoned in October of the same year.

ARIADNE continued to serve at Barrow during all these tribulations and was even reboilered in 1875 and her engines were compounded in 1885 by Westray, Copeland and Company of Barrow. At 36 years old she was finally broken up at Barrow in 1892.

Obituary notice

That the whole of the share capital of Anchor Line was eventually taken over by Swedish interests should bring a lump to the throat of any Englishman, let alone a Scot, who knows the history of this once illustrious line. No company better epitomised Scotland and the River Clyde. Its passenger carryings to the United States equalled such rivals as Cunard and Inman.

DOM PEDRO as ARIADNE, having lost her yards, with the distinctive cranes at Barrow-in-Furness in the background. *[Charles Dawson collection]*

IT TAKES ONE TO KNOW ONE

Ian Muir

Clydeside may not be the hub of shipbuilding and seaborne trade it once was, but the area remains one of the most active centres in Britain for professional and amateur interest in shipping. In senior position is the Institution of Engineers and Shipbuilders in Scotland dating from the fusion of earlier bodies in 1857, while of much more recent date are such as the Model Steamer Club, whose members entertain themselves - and large numbers of the public - by sailing their home-built radio-controlled miniatures in boating ponds throughout the area each summer. This article attempts to convey some of the colour and atmosphere of the monthly meetings of another such body, of which the writer was a member half a century ago.

Early in the Second World War his parents became friendly with a family who lived on the other side of the street at no great distance. Like father, John McNeilage fought his war from home, in his case because of his 'reserved employment'; that is to say he was considered of most worth to the war effort plying his trade. He worked for an upholstery contractor and the Lord alone now knows the hours John toiled fitting out warships and merchantmen on the Clyde and elsewhere, sometimes hammering home his last mouthful of tacks on a new vessel running trials, or making a furtive coastwise passage to join a convoy being marshalled in some darkened sea-loch who knew where. Likely that was small hardship, since it turned out he was a shipping enthusiast and scale modeller of Clyde pleasure steamers. Working from photographs and sketches, he produced his own character drawings of each subject then, by some black art, created their likeness in three dimensions with offcuts of wood, paper, and card such that the miniatures had the exact 'sit' of their full-size sisters. The models were waterline versions, however, and plied their routes only across the top of the display cabinet and piano - with wife Jean's tacit permission.

When the war was over, John announced that he was going to join the Clyde River Steamer Club (CRSC), which had resumed meeting; asking, as if he needed to learn, whether 'the boy would like to go?' He did, and he went. So did father for a few meetings, but soon found it all too intense, this enthusiasm. It was a feeling 'the boy' was to react to himself many years later but in those impressionable days of youth the Club provided a first experience of communal activity other than church organisations and school - though there were similarities. What a kenspeckle bunch the members were, and indeed remain!

The winter season monthly meetings of those post-war years were held 'within Room 6' on the ground floor of the Central Halls, Bath Street, Glasgow, at 7.30pm, for not to their devotees the relaxation and social intercourse of a yarn enjoyed over a pint in some hostelry. No, here the seating was prearranged in ordered rows and everyone faced the rostrum. The faded institutional decor of the place must have dated back at least two reigns, and undoubtedly owed something to Wesley or Calvin. Had anyone suggested an alternative venue of the type above they would have been shown the door, for sure. Was not one of the senior and most respected of the cognoscenti also a member of the Lord's Day Observance Society who, no matter the promised delights, foreswore all steamer excursions on the Sabbath?

Yes, these meetings were unashamed nostalgia trips for the male populace of Clydeside, personal comfort or the now much-peddled 'ambience' being a secondary consideration. Small wonder few women attended. Those who did were tweedy types mostly, and kept themselves unusually quiet. Fervour was the thing!

The assembly which gathered each winter month in these surroundings could easily have been taken for a cult meeting by some lost soul inadvertently pushing open the door and bursting in. Certainly it could not have looked as though enjoyment was the aim, but such was the case. A short-trousered seeker after knowledge who sat at the back gradually learned to recognise dyed-in-the-wool members, who would certainly have grumbled aloud had he arrived earlier and occupied their hallowed place in the fourth row, left, three seats out from the centre aisle.

Some minutes beyond the official starting time the eye of the hovering Chairman would lift to note several members entering together at the rear of the hall, signifying the safe arrival of a train bearing them from distant parts. Proceedings might now commence. These normally took the form of a lecture delivered by a senior member, and were illustrated by glass slides projected by what was still referred to as the 'magic lantern'. The instrument normally used was replete with polished brass fittings with knurled knobs for adjustment, and a blackened, distorted, ventilating chimney no longer as lightproof as its maker intended. Our reticent youth never ventured near enough to discover whether 'Galileo Fecit' was engraved thereon, but should not have been surprised to find it so.

Choosing his moment carefully the Chairman would attempt to introduce the speaker with just that degree of deference which he knew members expected of him. Things could go wrong at this early point however if Cataclysmic Cough was in his usual seat in the second row, extreme left. He wore a heavy dark blue belted coat and had haunted eyes and sunken cheeks which led the innocent observer to suppose his survival might be brief. Despite these dire symptoms he was a regular attender, arrived in good time, and

The LMS turbine DUCHESS OF MONTROSE dating from 1930 was the first vessel on which a sailing is remembered clearly, thought to have been at the Glasgow Fair holidays of 1942. Certainly, she was on the wartime Wemyss Bay - Innellan - Rothesay service, and bore us into the latter's bay which was by then alive with naval activities, not least the depot ship HMS MONTCLARE and her brood of submarines. Grey and rust-streaked, the DUCHESS had the air of a gracious but indigent gentlewoman somewhat incommoded by being obliged to wear her name abbreviated to D OF M'ROSE on fold-down 'convoy boards' attached to the upper deck rails so that her identity might be quickly denied to prowling periscope-peering predators. The second, civvy street view shows how attractive 'the MONTROSE' and her younger sister DUCHESS OF HAMILTON looked when in their true colours and well maintained. The former was a Denny product, 262 x 32 feet, with Parsons' three-shaft direct-drive turbines.

MARCHIONESS OF LORNE (bottom photograph, taken on 20th July 1950) was the third of the five disguised paddlers built for LMS Clyde services in the 1930s. If this affectation did anything for any of these ships then (in the writer's opinion) it probably detracted least from the little MARCHIONESS, whose appearance was squat but not displeasing. Built for the Holy Loch run in 1935, she did not need to go anywhere fast - which was just as well since her service speed was only 12 knots. Incredibly, the LMS went to the expense of a three-crank triple-expansion engine to produce this, a unit of $18\frac{1}{2}$, 29, and 45 x 48 inch being installed. Had it possessed a bit more power she might have lasted longer. Changed ways of working found her eventually on the Millport run where her inability to keep the timetable heaped public indignation upon her. Thus she served but nineteen seasons, being scrapped in 1955 at Port Glasgow. Her afternoon weekday waddle to Kilcreggan, Cove, Blairmore, Strone, Hunter's Quay, and Kilmun, providing an essential commuter service, had also offered war-weary Clydesiders the closest they could hope to get to a real peacetime steamer excursion. Her 'wee sail' was a discreet safety-valve, capable of being completed by tram and train from a Glasgow suburb between what Scots refer to as dinner and tea. Ship and machinery were by the Fairfield Shipbuilding and Engineering Co. Ltd., Govan. She was 199.5 x 27 feet.

would be affected early on by no more than what granny would have called a 'crechle'. The clearing of this minor irritation from the throat would only exacerbate the condition however, and by the time the Chairman took the floor members would be on tenterhooks lest repeated emphysemic eruptions eroded the enjoyment of the entire evening. With the closing words of the Introduction the ongoing muttered conversation three rows in front of the projector between Nervous Twitch and his summer cruising crony Thick Black would be stilled at last. Yet the meeting would remain conscious of the latter's presence throughout the evening since the outpourings of his briar could rival those of LORD OF THE ISLES when racing the mighty COLUMBA up Loch Fyne for Ardrishaig pier. So effective were his induced draught arrangements, the foul fug contained strong thermal upcurrents which imparted a spectral shimmering motion to the images of ships steaming along the lightbeam to the screen - and all eyes would be on it for members were a partisan lot. Old river rivalries died hard and when an impressive shot of some departed favourite was projected members so-minded signified their approval with a rumble of foot-stamping, though verbal disaffection by the unimpressed would have been thought unseemly - their turn would come!

But if there were those eccentric in habit and dress in the body of the meetings, surely the incurable cases were those who took the stand on successive nights. Encyclopaedic in knowledge, obese with timetables, they held us in their thrall - and surely none more fearsome in the full routh of reminiscence than the bush-browed, heavily jowled divine, the Reverend William C Galbraith, MA BSc. Jabbing the screen with a dominie's wooden pointer to ensure members missed not the interest and enjoyment latent in every rivet, he put a kink in the wake of successive steamers whose images staggered off course, transfixed. An impressionable tyro at the back could imagine the Reverend alter-ego thinking,

'There's how the MARCHIONESS likes her stake - straight through the boiler!'

His earthly dwelling was in the rarefied airs of Kelvinside Gardens, NW, a genteel precinct which the world's rush passed by, where antimacassars and aspidistras peeped from the bay windows of soaring terraces built in honey-coloured sandstone. You were really somebody in the Glasgow of those days if your house had bulged-oot windaes! He ministered to his flock nearby in St George's in the Fields, an impressive porticoed pile in the classical idiom which had been spared the Luftwaffe's fiery darts but was hit eventually by developers aiming a quick prestigious-flat conversion-package long after its latter-day Poundtext had been called to his last charge in Heaven. There, very likely, he thunders yet, addressing ancient Apostles on advances in navigation; and testing the patience of long-suffering Saints by holding forth upon the life and works of his personal paragon Dr John Inglis of Pointhouse Shipyard, builder of many swift pleasure steamers with a haystack boiler and single-diagonal engine.

At first it seemed fortunate not to be salvoed on Sundays by such a formidable presence, but the worthy minister must have had a softer side for in 1948 he penned a delightful booklet to mark the Diamond Jubilee of one of the kind - the writer's favourite steamer LUCY ASHTON. It was a gem then, is a collector's piece now, and at least one surviving copy is treasured still.

That great enthusiast Dan McDonald was best known as a stalwart of the CRSC's contemporary and rival, the Clyde Shiplovers and Modelmakers Society, of which he was a founder member. On one memorable occasion, however, he was asked to address a meeting of the former on his favourite topic, the Clyde puffers. Some people thought him self-effacing in company though found he shared his wide knowledge readily with those he knew well - but that night he demonstrated his mischievous streak. Years later he reminisced privately how he had enjoyed scandalising the douce, righteous, membership by asserting in forthright terms that '...with only seven inches of freeboard, the puffermen could expect a wet arse in wild weather.'

Save us, Dan, what an affront!

But the boy's favourite Steamer Club regular, and unwitting mentor, was the schoolmaster Ronald B McKim MA, on the staff of the German Department at Knightswood School on the city's north west periphery. Not for him the usual endless projection of views showing the same ship coming, going, passing and repassing; at every pier, perch, buoy, and beacon on the river. No, RB was a subversive heretic who once brought loud and irate shouts of 'This is a STEAMER club!' from the back of the hall when he had the black shameless bravado to show not one, not two, but sometimes more than three consecutive slides which did not depict favourites of the Firth! This gentle yet determined man might begin his excursion by leaving a hypothetical West-end tenement house to look first at the 'Glasgow Style' Art Nouveau stained glass of the stair-landing window, then marvel at the decorative ceramic-tiled magnificence of the 'wally close' before descending the entry's pipe-clayed steps to the pavement and approaching new-fangled electric tramcar which featured next. Splendid hilltop terraces by Charles Wilson, the Glasgow School of Art by Charles Rennie Mackintosh, Sauchiehall Street's Grecian Chambers by Alexander Thomson, and imposing works of other weel-kent Glasgow architects would be appraised with authority from the upper deck as the tram girned past towards one of the city-centre rail termini.

There we would arrive with time enough to admire the Manson bogie engine at the head of our boat-train at St Enoch, the 'Dunalastair' at Central, or attempt to penetrate the all-obscuring cloud of sulphurous reek that was Queen Street (Low Level) in the days of steam; depending upon which railway company's service to the coast we were to favour on that occasion. Eventually a slant of sunlight on the waters by the railhead pier would wake the fanatics from their torpor as the splash of colour on a steamer funnel emerging from a rain-blur was spied at last - just as the boy was revelling in the many other sights he was learning about in detail for the first time!

There must be few photographs which portray better what immediate post-war Clydeside was like. The day of overseas package tours, charter flights, and time-share in Spain were not quite with us. Everyone wanted to sail 'doon the watter', and in the view of QUEEN MARY II departing Glasgow's Bridge Wharf (top) a perceptible percentage of the population have pressed aboard with just that purpose in view. Even the fireman in the foreground by the accommodation scuttle has a smile on his face - and that with a few tons of coal still to shovel! Burns and Laird vessels lie opposite at the Broomielaw, themselves busy enough in the Irish trades. Dating from 1933, QUEEN MARY II was the last classic twin-funnelled three-shaft direct-drive turbine built for Clyde service, and the last to operate in the trade. Appropriately enough, she was a Denny product like the first of the kind, her running mate KING EDWARD. Latterly run with one funnel following the fitting of a Yarrow water-tube boiler, she now sports two again in her current role as a floating restaurant on the Thames.

It is a curious feature of Clyde steamer history that, despite being in the forefront of steam reciprocating engine development, steamer owners never attempted to produce a twin-screw passenger vessel for river services propelled by such means. Yet one such a ship did run for a single season. This was ROBINA, which David MacBrayne Ltd. chartered from Coast Lines Ltd. from June 1946 until the spring of 1948. She operated their twice-daily summer service from Gourock to Lochgoilhead in 1947 and one might have expected the venture to succeed since this sea route was direct and thought likely to be preferred by the fainthearted to the lengthy, circuitous, steep, and narrow route through the hills from Glasgow. Sadly, the venture was not a success, and was not repeated, and ROBINA is seen in June 1949 after she had left the Clyde. Built in 1914 and capable of around 14 knots, ROBINA was intended for excursions on the Lancashire coast, but had also seen service in the Bristol Channel and out of Belfast before arriving in the Clyde following the outbreak of war. She joined the fleet of tenders managed by the Caledonian Steam Packet Co. Ltd. at Gourock, and was thus well-placed to find employment when peace returned. *[World Ship Photo Library]*

The writer's parents had relations in Greenock and Helensburgh, periodic visits to whom throughout the war years providing a certain small boy with views of the Clyde's war effort from both banks. Usually these journeys from Glasgow were made by train, which in both cases afforded a better view of shipbuilding and repair yards than parallel bus routes through canyons of tenement dwellings. The earliest recollection of a river steamer is of LUCY ASHTON (top) at Craigendoran pier in 1940, pointed out by father when en route to visit his Helensburgh cousins. With her LNER sisters WAVERLEY, MARMION, TALISMAN, and JEANIE DEANS all away on war service, LUCY alone provided north bank steamer connections to Clyde piers. Built by T. B. Seath at Rutherglen in 1888, she was 190 x 21 feet, and propelled (since 1902) by a neat two-crank compound 28 and 52 x 60 inch diagonal engine by A. and J. Inglis of Glasgow, steam being provided by a coal-fired haystack boiler.

KING EDWARD (middle and bottom) of 1901 was the world's pioneer turbine-driven passenger steamer, providing at once the ability to steam farther and faster on day excursions for her owners while burning less coal. An immediate technical and commercial success, her 20.48 knots mean trial speed allowed her to outpace the fastest paddlers on a long run, though lack of comparable astern power put her at some disadvantage when manoeuvring at piers. Her First World War service took her as far as the White Sea, from which she returned unscathed. The Second World War was spent at home in the Clyde on public sailings and tendering duties to ocean liners at the Tail o'the Bank anchorage, but brought its own excitement. Before daylight, at 0700 on 21st October 1941, she

Yes, those imaginary excursions 'doon the watter' looked round and about, not solely at ships. Much was gained from them, a growing interest in architecture and railways, but not least breadth of vision. Sadly, Ronald McKim died but fifty-three, not long after learning of promotion to Head of Department. It was surely the poorer. His untimely death was certainly a sad loss to one avid listener - and perhaps to others who did not recognise theirs so plainly. His unshakeable aplomb, total command of his subject, and the assurance of his delivery in the face of Philistinism were object lessons that were to stand in good stead. They weren't all daft!

Whatever the intentions and expectations of the founders, there can be no doubt the body they created has exerted a civilising influence throughout its life. Real 'lantern lectures' still take place, and no member would consider a meeting brought to a close properly without the traditional Vote of Thanks to the Projectionist, '... whose support to the speaker has added much to our evening's enjoyment'. Long may the 'steamer dreamers' hold their course and speed!

had just departed Gourock on passage to Dunoon when she was struck on the port bow by the Burns and Laird Lines steamer LAIRDSBURN, inward bound from Ireland. The latter was not badly affected but the turbine steamer was cut to the keel, and beyond the midship line at promenade deck level, her mast being brought down. Beached in Cardwell Bay, just upstream of Gourock pier, KING EDWARD lay there for a time before moving to Port Glasgow for repair. Her severed degaussing cable can be seen (a wartime protection against magnetic mines), also her bow rudder which later saw service each evening when returning up-river astern on the last leg of her return to Glasgow's Bridge Wharf following the resumption of 'all the way' sailings to coast destinations on Saturday 1st June 1946. KING EDWARD was Denny built, 250.6 x 30 feet, and was propelled by Parsons direct-drive turbines on three shafts.

If LUCY ASHTON had been the Clyde's last surviving Victorian steamer, DUCHESS OF FIFE of 1903 proved to be its last Edwardian (this page). The latter was an elegant, popular, and successful steamer, having achieved 17.55 knots when contracted to produce 16. As DUKE OF FIFE she swept mines in the First World War, but kept her own name to repeat the process in the Second World War (top). Following a period laid-up off Kilcreggan in 1945, she arrived at James Lamont and Co.'s slip at Port Glasgow for return to public service. Side-slipped once out of the water, a thorough renovation was begun which was to last six months. The writer recalls seeing her several times from the passing train, funnel-less, and with large areas of daylight visible through the hull, such was the extent of shell plating renewal. Fortunately, someone left her convoy board attached to her bridge-wing stanchions throughout most of this, its ongoing assurance that the tangle of metal was in fact DUCHESS OF FIFE offering some hope for the future. That expectation was not misplaced. The middle photograph shows her ready for return to the water; the bottom one has her revelling in it as, with bunting aloft, she sets out from Port Glasgow to run trials on the Skelmorlie mile. Her machinery was interesting, being of the Rankin two-crank four-cylinder triple-expansion type; that is to say, the 35 and 52 inch IP and LP cylinders which were visible to the public were each backed by a hidden $16^1/_2$ inch diameter HP. Stephenson valve gear with long eccentric rods was fitted, placing the links just forward of the two larger cylinders. The wee FIFE was 210.3 x 25 feet, and in ship and machinery the Fairfield Shipbuilding and Engineering Co. Ltd. seldom built better. She was towed to Port Glasgow for scrapping in September 1953.

EVERY PICTURE TELLS A STORY

Last summer saw the sixtieth anniversary of the loss of HM Submarine THETIS commemorated in several articles, the fullest of which was John Shephard's in the June *Bulletin* of the Liverpool Nautical Research Society. John has sent this splendid photograph of the ZELO attempting to lift the THETIS.

ZELO was chosen to raise the THETIS as she was approximately the same length as the submarine, and at the time was at Cardiff on Admiralty charter. She was sent to Birkenhead where wooden lifting beams were fitted across her decks.

The photograph was taken on 22nd July 1939 and shows the second attempt to lift THETIS, which was abandoned when the wooden beams began to twist under the submarine's weight. ZELO returned to Birkenhead to have steel beams fitted, and returned in late August, when a series of lifts brought the THETIS high enough to be refloated with compressed air. As is well known, THETIS was refitted as HM Submarine THUNDERBOLT and was lost in the Mediterranean in March 1943.

The collier ZELO (2,294/1921) was built by S.P. Austin and Son Ltd. for the Pelton Steamship Co. Ltd. of Newcastle-upon-Tyne, and lasted in the fleet until 1955, when she was sold and registered in Costa Rica as KYRIAKOULA. After a brief spell as the Panama-registered PITSA, she was broken up in Greece in 1965. In the background is the salvage vessel RANGER (see page 190). *[Liverpool Nautical Research Society]*

With the classic backdrop of the Pool of London, and with lighters in the foreground, the Egyptian freighter MEMNON is assisted on her way with a deck cargo of truck or tractor tyres (below). This photograph from the late 1940s evokes a era that passed a quarter century ago - not only has commercial traffic gone from the Pool, but the skyline has been completely transformed by high rise buildings.

The oil-fired steamer MEMNON was built at Burntisland in 1947 for the Egyptian Shipping Co., and registered in Alexandria. Managers were the Euxine Shipping Co. Ltd. of London. MEMNON looks rather like a Baltic trader, and in 1950 she did pass to owners in the Baltic, being renamed BOREN under the Swedish flag. However, in 1954 she was back in the ownership of Euxine Shipping and under the British flag as HENDI. The small fleet of Euxine intrigues your editors, and would make an interesting short feature for *Record:* can anyone supply details of the company, its owners and trades?

When Euxine sold HENDI in 1962, a variety of flag-of-convenience owners operated her: an Italian who named her ERIKA, a Cretan who called her STEFANOS M, and a mainland Greek who named her VELBA and, for a few months, DIRFUS. She was broken up in 1976.

RECORD BOOKS
THE GENESIS OF WELSH MARITIME HISTORY
David Jenkins

In 1928, the University of Wales Press published the first of what was to become a series of annual St. David's Day booklets, comprising an essay, printed bilingually, that covered important events or significant individuals in the history of Wales. Intended primarily for secondary school pupils, the series rapidly gained popularity with the general reader, providing well-written and easily-understood introductions to some major themes in the history of Wales.

The series was interrupted by the Second World War, but the first post-war volume appeared in 1946. Three years later, in 1949, *Hen Longau a Llongwyr Cymru/Old Ships and Sailors of Wales,* by David Thomas, appeared. Produced in accordance with the austere standards of post-war publishing, it appeared to be a relatively unremarkable book, but in retrospect it can now be seen that this slim paperback volume was to prove a catalyst that not only ignited interest in Welsh maritime history, but which was to inspire subsequent researchers in their efforts.

It is somewhat ironic that its author, David Thomas, born in 1880, was brought up about as far from the sea as it is possible to get in Wales (!), in the Montgomeryshire village of Llanfechain, just a few miles from the English border. He had no seafaring ancestors whatsoever and pursued a career as a teacher, later becoming one of the pioneers of the Workers' Educational Association and the Labour Party in North Wales.

Thomas's introduction to maritime history came *via* John Glyn Davies, the remarkable, if somewhat eccentric, professor and head of the department of Celtic Studies at Liverpool University from 1920 until 1936. Davies had started his career in 1892 in the offices of the Liverpool-Welsh shipowners Thomas Williams and Co., owners of the famous Cambrian line of sailing ships; he also had strong connections with the Llŷn village of Edern, birthplace of Hugh Roberts, founder of the North Shipping Co. Ltd. of Newcastle, and of Owen and Watkin Williams, founders of Cardiff's Golden Cross Line. Thomas wished to undertake an MA degree, but was uncertain of a suitable study topic; it was Davies who suggested a socioeconomic study of maritime activity on the Llŷn Peninsula.

David Thomas researched his topic thoroughly and widely during the late 1920s, investigating documents in the Public Record Office and interviewing former seamen and shipowners living in retirement in Llŷn. He was duly awarded his MA in 1930. It was not until 1949, however, that Thomas published a more popular version of his research in the St. David's Day series, *Hen Longau a Llongwyr Cymru/Old Ships and Sailors of Wales.* In many ways, it is a somewhat sentimental volume;

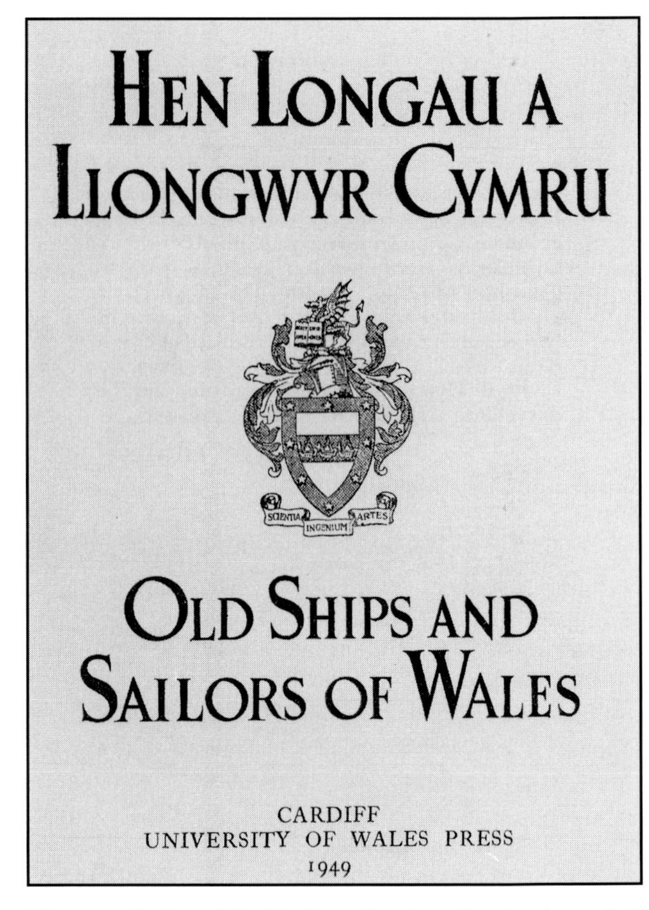

Thomas declared in his introduction that he intended to limit himself to the age of sail, and he spoke wistfully of '...the seaports of Wales...full of sailing vessels...each harbour seemed a forest of masts. Crowds of people and children watched them, with their sails filling in the wind, coming towards land, 'like doves to their cotes', a most beautiful sight'.

Nevertheless, the volume is significant in that it provides the only published continuous narrative of Welsh maritime history from the earliest times to the eve of the First World War. Though only some 10,000 words in length (in each language!), it touches deftly upon subjects as varied as medieval trade to the post-conquest castle towns, Elizabethan privateers, the gradual development of trade in the eighteenth century (spurred on by agricultural improvement and the Industrial Revolution) and wooden shipbuilding. Thomas concluded by looking at the intensity of maritime activity during the nineteenth century, when Welsh ships and seamen could be found in trades all over the world; slate to northern Europe, coal to the Mediterranean, copper ore from Chile and salt fish from Newfoundland.

Despite the wistful sentimentality shown by Thomas towards the age of sail, he readily acknowledged in the concluding pages of the book that the development of the steamship during the latter half of the nineteenth century was an inevitable progression that eventually brought about, '...new conditions at sea, safer ships and a better livelihood'. Whilst not everyone who sailed on a 'hard-case' Cardiff tramp during the inter-war years would have agreed with him, Thomas was nevertheless perceptive enough to realise that Welsh seafaring traditions were still evolving when the book was published in 1949; not for nothing was Blue Funnel, relying heavily upon masters and seamen from north Wales, known as 'the Welsh Navy', whilst Cardiff's Reardon Smith Line had a fleet of over twenty vessels at that time.

He concluded his book, however, by emphasising the importance of seafaring as a vital element in Welsh history. '...the charm and beauty of the old sailing vessels, and the adventurous spirit of their men, are part of the heritage of the Welsh nation, and we cannot afford to let them be forgotten. This little book has been written to help to keep their story alive'.

David Thomas's plea that Welsh ships and sailors should not be forgotten has not gone unheeded. In 1952, he himself published an exceptionally fine study (in Welsh) of the maritime history of Caernarfonshire, *Hen Longau Sir Gaernarfon.* Since Thomas's death in 1967, however, there has been a veritable avalanche of publications, in both languages, on Welsh maritime history, with the greatest contribution being made by one of Thomas's most dedicated admirers, the late Aled Eames. A lecturer in the University College of North Wales, Bangor, Aled described Thomas's publications as '....bright, but lonely lighthouses,' in the early days of Welsh maritime historiography, and they inspired him to write, or edit, over fifteen volumes on various aspects of the maritime history of north Wales and Liverpool, between 1973 and his untimely death in 1996. Also inspired by David Thomas's works was Lewis Lloyd, a lecturer at Coleg Harlech, and he produced a number of studies of individual ports in north and mid-Wales as well as an important volume on Welsh emigration to Australia. And in 1976, these two men came together with Bryn Parry, then Gwynedd's county archivist, to establish the journal *Cymru a'r Môr/Maritime Wales;* published annually since that date, it has been described as '. . . perhaps the best (journal) of its kind that we have seen... we heartily recommend it to all historians'.

It is difficult to imagine what David Thomas might have made of the current maritime scene in Wales: Cardiff *imports* coal and has just two shipping companies left; Liverpool no longer acts as a magnet for the seamen of North Wales; and whilst thousands of people go to sea for pleasure around the Welsh coasts, very few do so for profit. A seafaring tradition that evolved gradually over many centuries has all but disappeared in the space of half a century, and there is little likelihood of its revival in the near - or the distant - future. Nevertheless, the rich maritime history of Wales is still being recorded by a new generation of historians whose debt to the pioneering work of David Thomas remains as great as ever; whilst his legacy endures, there is no danger that it will be forgotten.

As a fitting accompaniment to David Thomas's book about maritime activity in Wales, Dr. David Jenkins has supplied this photograph of the Hugh Roberts' tramp steamer NORTH DEVON. To seek his fortune in the shipping business, the Llŷn-born Roberts did not migrate to Cardiff as did many of his contemporaries, but to Newcastle-upon-Tyne where he began shipowning in the 1870s. His North Shipping Co. Ltd. survived to be sold to Common Brothers in 1964.

NORTH DEVON (3,658/1924) was built and engined by John Readhead and Co. Ltd. at South Shields. Despite being bombed and damaged off Sheringham in July 1941, she survived the Second World War and is seen at Cardiff about 1948. In 1950 she was sold to the first of four distinct Greek owners, becoming the AGIOS SPYRIDON. In 1951, she sprang a leak whilst on a voyage from Huelva to Norresundby and was abandoned, but was later reboarded and taken into Brest. Her next owner named her THEOFOROS, and in 1954 converted her to oil fuel. In 1956 she became LENKO, in 1958 AIS GIANNIS, and as this was sold to Japanese breakers, arriving at Yawata on 15th May 1960. *[Hansen Collection 1987/2058; National Museums and Galleries of Wales]*

ON THE ROCKS

Peter Newall

Wrecks always seem to attract a ghoulish fascination, especially when there has been a large loss of life. But this is a selection of photographs of wrecked ships in which no one perished. All but two of the ships were later repaired and continued in service.

ORARA (top)
Blackwall, New South Wales; 1894, 66gt, 71 feet
ORARA was one of the numerous small steamers which served the various river ports on the north coast of New South Wales. Locally built, this wooden ship was owned by David Henderson of Grafton, a town on the Clarence River. The sand bars at the river mouths and the weather were constant problems for these ships and in February 1899 ORARA was wrecked at the entrance to the Tweed River whilst on a voyage from Sydney to the Tweed River with general cargo. *[Peter Newall Collection]*

NINGPO (middle)
Scott and Co., Greenock; 1898, 1,985gt, 275 feet
T. 3-cyl. by Scott and Co., Greenock
In the 1890s, Scott and Co. built a total of 24 ships for the China Navigation Co. Ltd. The managers of the company, Butterfield and Swire, had the virtual monopoly of the 'beancake' trade. Beancake, the pulp residue from soybeans, was an important fertiliser in southern China and NINGPO was one of many ships built specifically for this trade. A lucky ship, she survived mine damage in 1906 and going ashore on Shantung Promontory in the Yellow Sea in April 1921, as seen here. Refloated after the latter incident, and returned to service, she was sold for demolition in 1933. *[Peter Newall Collection]*

SHAN TUNG (bottom)
Taikoo Dockyard and Engineering Co. Ltd., Hong Kong; 1915, 2,549gt 310 feet
T. 3-cyl. by Taikoo Dockyard and Engineering Co. Ltd., Hong Kong
Another major expansion programme for China Navigation took place between 1914 and 1926 with over thirty ships being built, many from the company-owned Taikoo Dockyard. SHAN TUNG, one of a series of six coastal traders with 'S' names, was blown ashore at Swatow during a typhoon in August 1922. Four months later she was refloated and repaired. A survivor of the war, she was scrapped at Shanghai in 1948. *[Peter Newall Collection]*

CORCYRA (below)
Cook, Gemmell and Welton Ltd., Beverley; 1914, 225gt, 117 feet
T. 3-cyl. by Amos and Smith Ltd., Hull
Three months after her completion this Grimsby trawler, which was owned by the North Western Steam Fishing Co. Ltd., was taken over by the Royal Navy as a minesweeper. In February the following year she stranded off Bacton but was later salved. Her pennant number 278 can be seen roughly painted on the bow. During the Second World War she again saw war service, initially as an anti-submarine trawler and later as a water carrier. Despite her early misadventure, CORCYRA had a long life and, after returning to fishing, was broken up in Holland during 1961. *[Peter Newall Collection]*

CLEOPATRA (above and right)
Oregon Shipbuilding Corporation, Portland; 1944, 8,193 gt, 439 feet
Two steam turbines by the Westinghouse Electrical and Manufacturing Co., Pittsburg
In the late 1940s the Khedivial Mail Line purchased two former Victory ships and converted them into the passenger ships KHEDIVE ISMAIL (ex UNITED VICTORY) and MOHAMED ALI EL KEBIR (ex ATCHISON VICTORY). With a capacity of 134 in first class, the two ships were placed on the Egypt-USA service. In 1956 KHEDIVE ISMAIL was renamed CLEOPATRA and as such she ran aground at Gibraltar in good weather in June 1960. Suffering from serious damage to her bow she was later repaired but was subsequently withdrawn from North Atlantic service. She was sent to the breakers in 1981. *[Peter Newall Collection]*

TAK HING (top)
Kwong Hip Loong, Hong Kong; 1903, 617gt, 153 feet
C. 4-cyl. by Kwong Hip Loong, Hong Kong
The typhoon season in the Far East usually runs from June to October and on 18th September 1906 Hong Kong was hit by a devastating typhoon which caused major damage and many ships were thrown ashore including the river steamer TAK HING. Built by a Chinese-owned shipyard, she was owned briefly by the Hong Kong, Canton and Macao Steamboat Company, a long established line which operated passenger services between Hong Kong and mainland China. Sold 'as is' she was repaired and three years later was again damaged during a typhoon. She was eventually scrapped in the 1920s. *[Peter Newall Collection]*

DAKOTA (middle and bottom)
Eastern Shipbuilding Co., New London; 1905, 20,714gt, 630 feet
T. 6-cyl. by Midvale Steel Co., Philadelphia
At the opposite end of the size spectrum, DAKOTA and her sister MINNESOTA were among the largest ships of their day and when DAKOTA was wrecked near Yokohama in March 1907 she was the largest and most expensive merchant ship loss up to that date. Both vessels were ordered by the railroad tycoon James Hill, owner of the Great Northern Railway, from an east coast USA shipyard which had never built a ship before. Designed for a new service from Seattle to the Far East which would compete directly with the Vancouver-based 'Empresses' of Canadian Pacific, these giants were handsome ships with magnificent passenger accommodation but were hopelessly underpowered with a service speed of only 12 knots. DAKOTA struck a submerged reef but all 726 passengers were safely rescued. Three weeks later her remains sank after a storm. *[Peter Newall Collection]*

CANADIAN WOOD, U.S. STEEL

Captain Hubert Hall and Roy Fenton

The contribution of Canada to Allied merchant ship construction during the First World War was impressive. Despite the small size of the Canadian shipbuilding industry, it completed 44 wooden and 39 steel seagoing ships with 'War' names, according to Mitchell and Sawyer's *British Standard Ships of World War 1* (Journal of Commerce, Liverpool 1968). The fact that few were ready before the Armistice is more a reflection of British tardiness in ordering the ships than inadequacies of the industry.

Shortage of steel, much of which had to be imported from the USA, and an abundance of native timber encouraged the building of comparatively large wooden steamships. This was on a scale probably not seen before, and - given the very short lives of these vessels - it has not been repeated since for merchant vessels. On average, the wooden ships lasted under five years before being burnt out, wrecked, scrapped or hulked. Even those that were broken up or hulked had much shorter lives than the ten or twelve years their classification societies expected. One of the shortest lived was the WAR HALIFAX, seen here, which managed just one voyage before becoming one of no less than nine whose seagoing careers were terminated by fire. Only the WAR YUKON (2,242/1918) had a respectable career, trading until 1933 after which she was hulked before succumbing to the seemingly inevitable fire.

In contrast, the Canadian steamers built of US steel turned out to have satisfactorily long lives. Although the Second World War took its toll, several survived into the mid-1960s, including the WAR BEE built at New Glasgow, Nova Scotia and also featured here.

WAR HALIFAX
Southern Salvage Co. Ltd., Liverpool, Nova Scotia; 1918, 2,335gt, 250 feet
T. 3-cyl. by Robb Engineering Works Ltd., Amherst, Nova Scotia
The wooden shipbuilding industry in the Maritime Provinces during the latter part of the nineteenth century was on an enormous scale, with Prince Edward Island alone making a very significant contribution to the British fleet of sailing ships. It is therefore surprising that only two yards on the eastern seaboard of Canada built wooden steamers for the WAR programme, and their output was very limited. The sole contribution of the Southern Salvage Co. Ltd. of Liverpool was the WAR HALIFAX, launched during September 1918. Photographs of the wooden ships show a basically similar hull with engines aft of amidships, but with a variety of cargo gear.

Allocated by the Shipping Controller to Hansen Brothers and Co. Ltd. of Cardiff for management, WAR HALIFAX made just one voyage, and an expensive one for the British Government who paid the equivalent of £176,000 for her. WAR HALIFAX brought a cargo of timber from the port after which she took her name and safely delivered it to Barrow-in-Furness. She was then due to sail to the Baltic to load further timber. But calling at South Wales for bunkers, fire broke out in the 500 tons of coal aboard whilst she was in Roath Dock, Cardiff on 22nd October 1919, and it could only be extinguished by boring holes in her hull so that she sank. Considered not worth repairing, WAR HALIFAX was hulked and sold to Spain, after just one useful voyage. Her builders lasted no longer than the ship, and the Southern Salvage Co. Ltd. had gone out of business by mid-1919.

WAR WASP

WAR WASP

WAR WASP (opposite and this page top and upper middle)
Nova Scotia Steel and Coal Co. Ltd., New Glasgow, N.S.; 1917, 1,422gt, 220 feet
Steam turbine by DeLaval Steam Turbine Co., Trenton, New Jersey, USA.
A difficulty in manufacturing crankshafts in Canada led to some of the steel WARs receiving turbine machinery, something of an indulgence in a 220-foot tramp. However, these installations did not always prove satisfactory, and that in WAR WASP needed to be replaced in 1928. Following her sale by the Shipping Controller in 1919, she was sold to Compagnie Navigation Mixte to become CAPITAINE COULLON, but was resold within a year to Compagnie Génerale Transatlantique. The rather uneconomical machinery may have contributed to an early demise. CAPITAINE COULLON was sold to breakers in France in 1934, but was resold and actually broken up at Haulbowline near Cork early in 1936.

WAR WASP was launched on 9th July 1917, and is seen firstly on the ways with WAR BEE alongside, and immediately after her launch attended by the HIAWATHA, built at Pictou, Nova Scotia in 1904.

WAR BEE (lower middle) and **MÉCANICIEN MOUTTE** (bottom)
Nova Scotia Steel and Coal Co. Ltd., New Glasgow, N.S.; 1918, 1,730gt, 256 feet
T. 3-cyl. by the Nova Scotia Steel and Coal Co. Ltd., New Glasgow, N.S.
Although described as a sister to WAR WASP in one of the accompanying photographs, WAR BEE was in fact considerably longer and propelled by more conventional reciprocating machinery.

Her career did not start auspiciously: she was mined in the North Sea on 4th November 1918 on a voyage from Dunkirk to the Tyne. However, following her sale to Compagnie Navigation Mixte of Marseilles she had a long, if not entirely uneventful, career. As MÉCANICIEN MOUTTE she was seized by the Germans on 14th December 1942 and handed over to their temporary friends, the Italians who they were soon to turn on viciously. As CESENA the ship stayed out of trouble, partly because she was laid up at Barcelona in September 1943 and remained there until being handed back to her rightful owners in February 1945. She went back to Italy, this time legitimately, in 1949 as LAMONE, becoming PAOLETTO in 1960 and surviving until early in 1963 when her 45-year old hull was scrapped in Savona. *[All photographs Captain Hubert Hall collection]*

PUTTING THE RECORD STRAIGHT

Letters, additions, amendments and photographs relating to articles in any issues of *Record* are welcomed. Letters may be lightly edited.

EDWARD AURIOL: a vessel with a mission

This vessel (*Record* 10, page 102) was built by Edwin Clark and Co., Brimscombe (not Clard) as their yard number 14. Built purely as a mission vessel, with no towing facilities, she was presumably converted to a tug in 1911 after being sold out of mission service. She was fully written up in the *Marine Engineer* for 1st January 1889, pages 345-6, complete with drawings of the hull and steam engine and a full specification.

EDWARD AURIOL was delivered to London under her own steam via the Stroudwater Navigation, the River Severn, the River Avon, the Kennet and Avon Canal, and the River Thames. After arrival she was dedicated by the Bishop of London at a church service on 28th November 1888. She plied between London Bridge and the Nore distributing bibles and other items to the crews and emigrants on outward and homeward bound vessels, and helping to arrange services on board these ships.

In the same article, PRIVATEER was built by Thomas and William Toward. TOPMAST No.1 was in fact built for the War Office as a miner, named PENNAR, not coming into Admiralty ownership until 1905 when renamed HMS NETTLE. She was J. Samuel White yard number 1152, and received the official number 400031 in Ireland.

BRIAN HILLSDON, 72 Marlborough Road, Ashford, Middlesex TW15 3PW.

Matters arising from *Record* 9 . . .

As well as the Commonwealth Conference it was also the quite separate New Zealand Conference that Blue Star did the breaking into - for southbound loading only until 1958 (page 17, first paragraph). Shaw, Savill and Albion was acquired by Furness Withy in 1933, not 1935. It was the White Star Australian services that were purchased in 1935.

The claim that the ship on the left of the bottom photograph on page 19 is a British Phosphate Commission ship is incorrect. It is actually SUVA, (4,873/1938), built by Bartrams at Sunderland for W.R. Carpenter and Co. Ltd.

On page 26 and 27, a comment could have been made that WELLINGTON STAR and AUCKLAND STAR of 1939 were the first to have kingposts on the forecastle. Not all the previous ships had straight bar stems: the two just mentioned and AUCKLAND STAR had soft-nosed stems, although the curve of the stem was not as pronounced as in the post-war pair. EMPIRE STAR on page 28 was a Shaw, Savill and not a Blue Star design.

I have a copy of the photo of SAINT RONANS on page 40 and believe the ship is indeed in Rankin, Gilmour's colours. At that time the red band tended to be darker than the red of the funnel base. The JACATRA (page 41) was definitely laid down for Rankin, Gilmour as SAINT THEODORE.

Although I have never seen it before, I believe the photograph on page 43 is Strick's ARABISTAN of 1893 on trials in the Clyde - one can almost discern the Stephen's houseflag at the main.

The reference to Royal Rotterdam Lloyd on page 61 is anachronistic. In 1920 it was plain Rotterdam Lloyd, not becoming Royal until 1947.

The AMBULOMBO as MANOORA (page 64) ran between Sydney and Fremantle only during the summer months. During the winter she ran between Melbourne and Cairns.

BILL LAXON, Waimarama, Upper Whangateau Road, PO Box 171, Matakana 1240, New Zealand.

EDWARD AURIOL photographed at Brimscombe by the builder's wife just before her delivery voyage (right). *[Brian Hillsdon collection]*

Bill Laxon's identification of the ARABISTAN as the Clyde-built vessel of 1893, is confirmed by the presence of the original negative amongst the trials photographs held by Glasgow University. Taken in Wemyss Bay, it shows the ship in pristine condition, flying a name pennant, and with the name ARABISTAN clearly visible on the bow. Like the print used in *Record* 9, this has Strick's chevrons pointing the wrong way, presumably because of a painting error. Suggestions that this is because the photograph is printed the wrong way round can be dismissed: if it was, the chevrons would still point towards the bows! *[University of Glasgow DC101/0031]*

. . . and *Record* 10

The caption for the ROBERT L. HOLT (*Record* 10, page 71) says that she was the only one of the 1926 trio lost during the Second World War, but CACHAPOAL (ex-HALSTEAD, ex-JONATHAN C. HOLT) was wrecked on 11th April 1945. I know she was a marine rather than a war loss but it still happened during the period of the War.

The first photo caption (page 88) says that the LINNET is on the port side of the PATROCLUS whereas she is, of course, on the starboard side. The sailing barge outboard of the LINNET is the THISTLE of Rochester, a topsail coasting barge built by George H. Curel at Frindsbury in 1888 and owned in 1907 by Henry Attwood of Portland, Dorset. On 30th March 1912, while on a voyage from London to Poole with barley, the THISTLE struck Portsmouth boom defence and sank although her crew of three were saved. The wreck was subsequently refloated and converted into a lighter at Portsmouth, renamed CAN, and owned by Camper and Nicholson Ltd. She drops out of the *Mercantile Navy* List in 1930.

BOB TODD, National Maritime Museum, Greenwich, London SE10 9NF.

Silvers from Sunderland

In part 2 of the series on two-funnel cargo liners (*Record* 8) it states that the Silver Line had ordered three further turbine vessels to follow on from the SILVERBRIAR and SILVERPLANE. Actually, four ships were ordered. The first, third and fourth were sold to Alfred Holt whilst the second ship was sold to the Indo China Steam Navigation Co. Ltd. and named EASTERN GLORY. These ships were slightly smaller than the first two, and did not have the trunked hatch to No. 3 hold. The composite deckhouse had a large and imposing single funnel which gave these ships the appearance of being true Blue Funnel vessels. The EASTERN GLORY had a similar funnel. Although very close family connections existed between the owners and J.L. Thompson, the shipbuilders, Silver Line did not own the yard as was stated.

ADAM SCOTT GRAY, 27 Glenesk Road, Sunderland, SR2 9BN.

As a follow-up to our 'British Yards, Greek Tramps' article, Adam Scott Gray has provided much extra detail about the Greek tramps built in Sunderland, which we hope to include in a future article.

DUKE becomes JOHANNA

A minor point regarding DUKE OF NORFOLK on page 111 of *Record* 10. On page 68 of *Marine News* for March 1968 Rodger Haworth provided a fleet list for Eastern Steamship Co. This provides an additional name in her later career, as the Swedish JOHANNA of Rederi A/B Banco (C.J. Banck) between 1908 and 1914. Her loss as the Greek PERICLES was on her maiden voyage for her new owner.

GEORGE ROBINSON, 7 Hornbeam Walk, Cottingham, East Yorkshire HU16 4RS.

ARCs, Indiamen and Liberties

At the time Trader Navigation purchased ARCTEES, following the death of Sir Joseph Isherwood (*Record* 9, page 4) there were, in addition to the three arcform ships trading, a further two on order to be named ARCSCOTT and ARCROWAN. They were sold and completed in 1938 as MOUNT IDA for Rethymnis and Kulukundis and WRAY CASTLE for Chambers.

The article on Trader comments on the short period many of the ships were retained before sale. This may be a reminder of the different climates of liner and tramp trades. Liner companies had two goals: profit and maintaining a service. Tramp owners had only one: profit. Though some tramp owners retained their ships for long periods, there were two profit opportunities open to them. First, there was profit earned on freights; second, profit from buying and selling ships. The second could be as lucrative as the first. In my *Nitrate Boats*, Appendix 5 suggests Sir John Latta made a profit of some 12% on the sale of ships.

In the case of Trader, being a private company owned totally by Bunge, accounts are unlikely to be

Built by William Hamilton and Co. Ltd. at Port Glasgow, MOUNT IDA (4,202/1938) was intended to be ARCSCOTT, one of Sir Joseph Isherwood's ARCFORM ships. The upper photograph shows the Greek-registered steamer at Tilbury on 29th May 1939, towards the end of her tragically short life. On 10th October 1939 she was wrecked on Ower Bank, east of Cromer, whilst on a voyage described as being from Vancouver to Leith with a cargo of grain, lumber and metal. Her crew were rescued by the Cromer Lifeboat H.F. BAILEY. By a remarkable coincidence, two years later the same lifeboat was rescuing survivors from another of the five ARC ships, the ENGLISH TRADER ex-ARCTEES, which was wrecked on Hammond Knoll in 1941 (see *Record* 9, page 5 and *Record* 1 page 53). *[P.A. Vicary, courtesy World Ship Photo Library collection]*

The last of the original five ARC ships was intended to be ARCROWAN, but was launched by William Hamilton and Co. Ltd. as WRAY CASTLE (4,253/1938) for J. Chamber's Lancashire Shipping Co. Ltd. (lower photograph). WRAY CASTLE was sunk by the German submarine U 103 on 3rd May 1941 whilst on a voyage from Mauritius to Freetown with a cargo of sugar. Both ships had triple-expansion engines by David Rowan and Co. Ltd. *[World Ship Photo Library collection]*

Like the LINNET (*Record* 10, page 89) the salvage steamer RANGER was originally a warship. She was built and engined in 1880 by John Elder and Co. at Govan as a composite gun vessel, but was sold out of service in September 1892. The Liverpool Association for the Protection of Commercial Interests as Respects Wrecked and Damaged Property registered her in their home port in 1893. A re-engining by Workman, Clark in 1904 assured her of a long life, and she was not broken up until 1954, when Henry Bath and Son Ltd. dismantled her in Salthouse Dock.

available. But were they so, a compilation of first cost, freight profits, depreciation and sale prices would allow an interesting analysis.

In *Record* 10, pages 88-9 include pictures of LINNET working on the PATROCLUS casualty. It is interesting to compare her with the better known RANGER: both came from the same cradle, gunboats converted to salvage vessels. The story of the Liverpool Salvage Association must be a most interesting one; I recall their Secretary telling me that the composite hulls of RANGER and LINNET enabled them to be squeezed into dangerous positions and come out without damage.

The article on DRONNING SOPHIE calls her an East Indiaman. I have always understood East Indiamen were owned or chartered by the Honourable East India Company (HEIC), heavily armed and with large crews. Years before DRONNING SOPHIE was built in 1847 the HEIC lost its monopoly, and in 1834 withdrew from commerce and limited its interests to governing India. The fleet of Indiamen was sold and trade opened to all. Afterwards the nearest to an Indiaman was the more economical Blackwall frigate built after 1837. Hence DRONNING SOPHIE was merely a cargo vessel built in Burma for an Indian owner, not the HEIC.

Page 26 has reference to DORINGTON COURT in the ancestry of the emergency ships built during the war. I recall Thompson staff from the time saying the plans taken to America were those of EMPIRE LIBERTY. Thompsons came out of the depression with EMBASSAGE of 1935, first of a design that developed through DORINGTON COURT (which impressed the Admiralty with her speed/power ratio), to EMPIRE LIBERTY and eventually the Oceans and Liberties. The visual differences are details on what is basically the same ship.

DAVID BURRELL, 63 Avisyard Avenue, Cumnock, Ayrshire KA18 3BJ.

Counter claims

The comment in the caption to the JOHN HOLT in *Record* 10 that she and her sister ship ‘may have been unique amongst post-war newbuildings in having counter sterns’ is true only insofar as British shipping companies and shipyards were concerned.

The liners CONSTITUTION (23,719/1951) and INDEPENDENCE (23,719/ 1950) of American Export Lines were almost certainly the last vessels to sport this design and followed on from a series of counter-stern freighters owned by this company; precursors and variants of the American standard C3 design built before and during the Second World War. Johnson Line too had incorporated this elegant feature in a series of twin-screw motor cargo ships built during the 1940s, with the last example GUAYANA being delivered by Götaverken A/B as late as 1948. The BOLIVIA, completed in the same year as the two Holt vessels referred to above, survived these by some measure and was not broken up until 1979.

With regard to the subsequent history of FLORENCE HOLT, it would seem that she did not carry

quite as many names under the various manifestations of Mr. Scufalos's ownership as recorded in the fleet list. As the TRIAS she spent the best part of 1973 languishing on a lay-by mooring in the Rijnhaven at Rotterdam, with the name barely discernible on the heavily rusted hull. Whilst for the latter part of the period *Lloyd's Shipping Index* noted that she was to be renamed DAYTON, her next movement at the end of that year - which was to take her to the breakers at Kaohsiung via Mormugao and Singapore - was made as the MR NORMAN and it is unlikely that the name DAYTON was ever carried. Despite being broken up at the beginning of 1974, she was still listed in the 1974-75 Register as MR NORMAN, which tends to confirm that no further change of name was made. Confusingly the sales section of *Marine News* for May 1974 (page 206) records an initial change of name to DAYTON and then MR. NORMAN, although the former name is not mentioned in the 'demolitions' entry of the same issue (page 212). A sad end to the fine ship, whatever.
PAUL BOOT, 29 Meadowcroft, Heswall, Wirral, Cheshire CH60 1UT.

WENDOVER's windows

Like your other correspondents who sailed on more traditional cargo liners of the day, I have to admit to having had a certain lordly disdain tinged with a considerable degree of envy for Watts, Watts' WENDOVER class (*Record* 6). Many years later I worked with a chap who had been a superintendent with Watts, Watts and he told me about those windows along the ship's side. Edmund Watts was a pretty forthright character and having decided he wanted something, he was going to get it. However good the windows were for crew welfare, they were not good from the point of view of contemporary naval architecture. Lloyd's Register was very concerned about so many holes in the sheer strake, a prime strength member of the ship's hull, and the resulting loss of strength. Edmund Watts insisted and the problem was overcome by increasing the thickness of the sheer strake in the area concerned. This would have incurred the penalty of an increased light ship weight and also a higher building cost. Lloyd's Register covered themselves by insisting that the steelwork was inspected frequently, at Watts, Watts' expense, to check that no cracks were developing from the corners of the window apertures. This must have been quite a performance.
KEN GARRETT, 3 The Grange, East Malling, Kent ME19 6AH

DURAS at Portavogie

The DURAS (*Record* 7, page 185, and *Record* 10, page 103) was named after the home of the chairman of the Congested Districts Board, Major J. Wilson Lynch, which was just outside Kinvarra in south Galway. The Board was set up to relieve unemployment and help the poor in the west of Ireland. DURAS was replaced in 1912.

In 1936 she was bought by W. and A. McMullan Ltd., Portaferry and William A. Glenn of Portavogie. Under the command of the latter she traded regularly from Ardrossan, Irvine, Troon, Ayr, Maryport and Whitehaven to Irish ports from Donaghadee in County Down as far as Skerries and Balbriggan in County Down. She was a regular visitor to Strangford Lough, and would be found in Portaferry, Strangford Lough and Killyleagh, and the now-defunct ports of Ringhaddy, Castle Elspie, Ballydorn,

Johnson Line sold the BOLIVIA in 1971 to Compania Naviera Americana de Vapores S.A. (which appears to be an Argentinean subsidiary of Ybarra) and she remained in their service as the BALBOA, as which she was photographed on the Clyde in 1978. Paul Boot reports that she had visited the UK running on the BHLR conference service and had sailed from Liverpool the previous evening in foul weather. Hence Paul's trip to the Clyde.

Sold to Compania Tarragona de Naviera S.A. in 1978 and renamed SHAHEEN I, she survived as such for only a few months and arrived at Karachi on 12th January 1979 for demolition by Haji & Co. *[Paul Boot]*

Quoile Quay, and Kircubbin. She was often found discharging in the small ports of the Solway Firth, such as Garlieston, Isle of Whithorn, Port William, and Drummore, and - on the other side of the Mull of Galloway - discharging in Stranraer. Her cargoes included coal, timber, cement, bricks and potatoes.

On Sunday, 3rd September 1939, the day war was declared, she sailed from Maryport for the last time bound for Drummore in Wigtonshire. None of her crew was ever back in Maryport again. In July 1940 she was taken over by the Admiralty and worked in Belfast Lough under the command of William Glenn.

The DURAS is remembered with great affection here in Portavogie. The ship and her captain were household names amongst the old seafarers of the village. With her sale in October 1942, so passed the last merchant ship owned in Portavogie.

CAPTAIN JAMES MOOR, En Casa, Cloughey Road, Portavogie, Newtownards, County Down BT22 1EF.

Details of the career of DURAS appeared in Record 7. *Ed.*

Wrong four-master

On page 110 of *Record* 10 the comment is made that the STAFFORDSHIRE of 1894 was the first Bibby four-master to have her mainmast stepped on the boatdeck just forward of the bridge. I would claim that the CHESHIRE and SHROPSHIRE of 1891 were the first. Dimensions of the STAFFORDSHIRE in *Lloyd's Register* show her to be almost identical but with more powerful engines and photographs show the same general layout.

The claim for the STAFFORDSHIRE may possibly be connected with a frequently-published photograph claiming to show the CHESHIRE in Colombo Harbour. The ship has her mainmast stepped on her foredeck. The catch is that the port bears no resemblance at all to Colombo (I sailed there frequently courtesy of Clan Line) and the ship is not the CHESHIRE. Examination of the signal flag hoist shows LJCB of the YORKSHIRE of 1889 and not the CHESHIRE (MHBW) of 1891 in the International Code of 1857-1900.

The port is clearly in the Mediterranean and my guess is that it is Brindisi. I wonder what happened to the real photograph of the CHESHIRE in Colombo Harbour?

M.J.M. BEDFORD, 3 Clareville Grove Mews, Clareville Street, London SW7 5AN

Mr. Bedford supplied excellent photographs of YORKSHIRE, and we are holding these over for a Fleet in Focus feature on the Bibby four masters in a forthcoming Record. *Ed.*

PARADISE found

In the fleet history of Tower & Ensign Express Shipping in *Record* 8 under TOWER DUCHESS appears: 3.1984: Sold to R.B. Berkshire, St. John's, Newfoundland and renamed PARADISE SOUND. Continued existence doubtful (1998). The ship indeed does still exist. I talked with a friend who is captain of a tug which arrived at Arnold's Cove, Newfoundland in November. R.B.(Ray) Berkshire lives at Arnold's Cove so I asked my friend if there were any other ships there. He said yes, there was a coastal freighter docked nearby and her name was PARADISE SOUND. She is still used by Ray Berkshire in various trades on the Newfoundland/Labrador coasts. He also owns a wooden doubled-ended freighter built 1964 in Newfoundland named BEOTHIC VENTURE which has recently been given a coat of fibreglass over the hull - a practice common here with older wooden hulls.

HUBERT HALL, PO Box 476, Yarmouth, Nova Scotia, Canada B5A 4BY

From sterns to wheelhouses

Record 10 arrived yesterday - better than ever - truly! May I make a few comments?

Pages 74-75. I remember seeing an immaculate JOHN HOLT crossing the Liverpool Bar inward as we were bound out, some time in 1952, and was astonished when the pilot told me she was only six years old. That counter stern gracing JOHN and ROBERT L. HOLT must have been the last built into any British ship and probably the only ones post 1945. The only other two counter sterned post-war ships I can recall were the American Export Lines' INDEPENDENCE and CONSTITUTION, at least one of which I believe to be still afloat. I never sailed with a counter stern myself but was told by apprentice pals of mine who did that sure, they looked pretty, but were the very devil to chip rust off!

Page 84. Nice picture, but I searched in vain for a floating dock such as I have always known them - a floating dry-dock - then realised I was seeing a picture of a dock in which vessels floated at all states of the tide.

Page 86. I know an old engineer (actually a very active lad of 86) who sailed with Scott-Still engines. He describes them as the supreme manifestation of the fact that oil and water do not mix. Brilliant idea on the drawing board but absolute horrors to work.

Page 88. PATROCLUS has what I was told early in my career was a 'West Hartlepool wheelhouse' - clearly shown on those marvellous photographs. From ahead it looked like a real wheelhouse but it was only a screen, leaving all on the bridge otherwise totally unprotected from the elements.

CAPTAIN A.W. KINGHORN, 15 Kendal Avenue, Cullercoats, North Shields, Tyne and Wear NE30 3AQ.

LANCING at Melbourne

I can confirm the photograph of LANCING on page 112 of *Record* 6 was taken in Melbourne. She is berthed at what is now known as No 16 South Wharf. Unfortunately I cannot date the visit. Congratulations on a first class publication.

LINDSAY REX, 57 Dalgetty Road, Beaumaris, Victoria 3193, Australia

Facts by phone

Bill Harvey called to suggest that the unknown tug belonging to William Cooper shown in the photograph on page 93 of Record 10 is the HALLGARTH (74/1895). Built at Lytham for R. and J.H. Rea Ltd. as CUMBRIA, she became HALLGARTH in 1899 when a new form of nomenclature was adopted using names of farms in the Lake District. HALLGARTH was bought by the Admiralty in March 1900 and kept her civilian name although she was additionally known as C62. In September 1941 she was sold to the Southern Salvage Co. Ltd. of Salcombe, but just two months later passed to Coopers. HALLGARTH's register was closed in 1951, presumably on her being broken up. HALLGARTH was a near-sister to FELLGARTH, shown in Record 3, page 140.

Peter McNicol doubts that Blue Funnel's ASCANIUS (3) was the last coal-burning troopship (see Record *10 page 87). He witnessed the EMPIRE TEST (8,298/1922) coaling at Mombasa in February or March 1951. The twin-screw EMPIRE TEST was the former Belgian THYSVILLE, which came under British control in 1940 but was not renamed until 1947. Mitchell and Sawyer record that she made her last voyage in October 1952, after which she was broken up at Faslane. According to* Lloyd's Register *she was a coal burner until the end.*